CALLED BY A NEW NAME

BECOMING WHAT GOD HAS PROMISED

CALLED BY A NEW NAME

BECOMING WHAT GOD HAS PROMISED

BY

GERRIT SCOTT DAWSON

UPPER
ROOM BOOKS
NASHVILLE

Called by a New Name

Upper Room® Web address: http://www.upperroom.org

UPPER ROOM®, UPPER ROOM BOOKS™ and design logos are trade-
marks owned by The Upper Room®, Nashville, Tennessee. All rights
reserved.

Scripture quotations not otherwise identified are from the New Revised
Standard Version Bible, copyright © 1989 by the Division of Christian
Education of the National Council of the Churches of Christ in the U.S.A.
Used by permission.

One scripture identified *New International Version* is from the *Holy Bible,
New International Version*. Copyright 1978 by the New York International
Bible Society. Used by permission of Zondervan Bible Publishers.

Cover Art Direction: Michele Wetherbee
Cover Design: Marc Tedeschi
Cover Photograph: © 1994 Shelly Firth
Interior Design and Layout: Nancy Cole
Second Printing: 2000

Library of Congress Cataloging-in-Publication Data

Dawson, Gerrit Scott.
    Called by a new name: becoming what God has promised / by Gerrit
Scott Dawson.
        p.   cm.
    Includes bibliographical references.
    ISBN 0-8358-0802-5 (pbk.)
        1. Christian life. 2. Names. Personal—Religious aspects—
Christianity. I. Title.
BV4501.2.D392   1997
    248.4—dc20

                                                                96-30406
                                                                CIP

Printed in the United States of America

For Steve Strickler

Your name means "Friend" to me.

CONTENTS

INTRODUCTION

What's in a name?
— Shakespeare, "Romeo and Juliet"

What names have you been called in your life? Many people snicker when I ask that question. They're thinking, perhaps, of some of the unflattering nicknames that stuck to them long ago in school. Or they're recalling some of the words that flew last week during a squabble at home.

But when I ask them to think back more positively, quite often their faces soften. They remember the love in nicknames from parents and close friends. A memory surfaces of being held on a grandparent's lap and called by a special name. Some recall adults who showed affection by making gentle sport of our names. Those who have children now smile for the intimacy of the pet names that are used in loving families. Names communicate relationships between people, and so reflect our basic identity.

We've also been called by names which denote our function in the world. One person can be simultaneously "Mom," "CPA," and "deacon." In those three names we can discover how that particular woman spends most of her time, what her priorities and skills are, and how her external, daily life is perceived by the world. Names help us find our place.

Our given names are also full of meaning for us. For better or worse, we are connected by name to those who went before us. Some bear the burden of heritage. Others consider how they are spiritually related to the biblical character after whom they were named. This connection may be strengthened if one received a special new name at confirmation or baptism. Research into our given names may uncover meanings and history we never had before. We each relate to our particular names as popular or rare, contemporary or old-fashioned. We are shaped by the names given to us, and they locate us within a particular culture, faith, and family heritage.

Such proper names, titles, and nicknames are quickly discerned and provide a reading on our place in the world. We have other names, however, which are not as easily recognized but still exert a powerful influence upon us. These are our inner names, the descriptions of our value and place in the world. They may be phrases rather than proper names. Though seldom spoken aloud, these names describe the way we perceive the current state of our lives. What name fits you now?

For instance, if you are a harried care-giver, your name these days might be, "Always on Call." But if you're wondering where your loved ones are, you might choose "Waiting by the Phone." During a busy season at work, you might be "My Office, My Home." Or a parent with a house full of children (and dishes) might select "Still Standing at the Sink."

On a deeper level, you might realize that the name that describes you is "Alone Again." Another's name in a season of joy might be "A Heart Full of Love." "Irrelevant" could be the choice for someone who feels unable to make her voice heard anymore. Or a man might pick "On the Run" for all the ways he stays busy to keep from thinking. The name for the current condition of your life might be as simple as "Harvest," "Stressed Out," "Thankful," or "Weary."

Of course few of us actually go by the names which describe us. But we do live under their power. Our inner names are the ways we think of ourselves. They shape our expectations of what our portion in life is to be, and so they influence our daily circumstances. One whose inner name is "Dead End" finds that new possibilities for growth rarely arise, while one whose name is "Smooth Sailing" seems always to have a knack for turning difficulties into blessings.

We receive these names from circumstances and especially from our most significant relationships. Those who love us name us as "Needed" or "Cherished" and so give us the strength to carry on. But old voices from long ago may threaten to drag us down. They say our names are "Always At Fault" or "Too Smart for Your Own Good," or "In the Way." When those names are called, we answer to them and fulfill our expected roles.

CHANGING YOUR NAME

Ideally, we would like to quiet the old, diminishing names and live more fully from the affirming names. For years now, self-help books have encouraged us to do just that. We are taught to change our inner picture of ourselves to improve everything from work to relationships. We've been told in essence to pick a better name and live accordingly. If you don't like the name of your life, change it! Dismiss the old negative names, and embrace the new positive ones.

But for any who have tried, such change is much easier

said than done. The old names are very persistent. And so questions arise: By whose authority may I change my name? How do I find the power to silence the old names which seem so apt? What hope is there that I will live up to a new name? Obviously, we will need a power greater than ourselves if we are to embrace new, life-giving names with confidence. More than mere wishful thinking, it would be of great help to discover the names God gives us.

This brings up the dimension to our consideration of names that is deeper than the latest techniques in self-improvement. What names does God call us, both individually and as the community of his people? If a name is a leading image that communicates a measure of worth and function, then how is God seeing us? We would like very much to know, because a name given by God would come to us with the authority of the Creator. It would offer us ways to think of ourselves, confidently and constructively, based on the way God thinks of us. A title from God would provide direction to our work in the world, and define our life in the community of believers.

NEW NAMES FROM GOD

Throughout the Bible we can find descriptions of the ways God sees us and names us. But especially in the third section of the book of Isaiah, we discover sets of beautiful new names promised to the people who were undergoing disgrace and exile. These names are for us today as well. They give us hope that like the people of God in Isaiah's day, we may be "re-named" also no matter our circumstances.

The different names promised in Isaiah address three aspects of life. First, several of them name our essential identity as God's beloved children. These names are given in contrast to the names of brokenness the world has given us. They reach our ears with the pleasant sound of names spoken by those who love us most. Second, other names call forth our primary tasks in daily life. They provide us the titles under which we engage in meaningful service for God. They name us as those who work with God in restoring the world. And third, there are names that place us in community with others. They locate us in the culture of God's people who have a great word of hope for the world.

If we could receive these names from God, then we might begin to think of ourselves, and our communities of faith, in new ways. We could imagine our lives not only according to present circumstances but according to the promises of God's future, which begin to come to be right now. So we could discover that we are not merely what others call us, nor bound forever to what life has done to us. We are not what our circumstances attempt to dictate. We are what God names us to be. And we can become more and more what God has promised to make us in these names. Then we discover that the freedom of such names is meant to extend to everyone. God is renaming the creation.

This book is an invitation to discover what God names you and to take those names as your own. First, we will consider the diminishing names placed upon us and how we may be free of them. Then we will explore each of the names promised in the third part of Isaiah and discover how we too may receive the blessing of such names.

The new names are a gift of God's grace, made available as a result of God's own work of redemption in Jesus Christ. We may have them only because God graciously chooses to give them. But our part in receiving them nevertheless remains crucial. Throughout these chapters, we will explore how the use of our imagination in prayer and reflection enables us to accept the names God offers us. And by the end, we will have learned how we may live daily under the power of these names in confidence and joy.

In the same way that we receive the new names by God's grace, so do we know of God only by gracious revelation. God does not exist in our image; we are made in God's image. God is neither male nor female. Rather, God is all that male is (and more) and all that female is (and more). Only together, as male and female, do we humans approach being the image of God we were meant to be. Pronouns that imply gender in God are, as all words describing God, inadequate. Yet, we need pronouns in writing to express the intimacy of the relationship between God and humanity, which we find in the new names. Moreover, the scriptures, the language of revelation, grant us pronouns for God. And, these pronouns are masculine. So you will find them in this book. They are used, however, always with an awareness that it is God's self-giving love in Jesus Christ that sets the terms for our lives and our language.

I am most grateful to the congregation and study groups of the First Presbyterian Church of Lenoir and to the Western Ohio School of Ministry (United Methodist). Their interest helped shaped these pages. I am also indebted to J. Alec Motyer's brilliant commentary *The Prophecy of Isaiah*, which has formed the critical foundation of this work.

— GERRIT DAWSON
Holy Monday, 1996
Lenoir, North Carolina

PART ONE

———•◦◆◦•———

PREPARING
FOR THE
NEW NAMES

CHAPTER 1

THE NAMES OF DIMINISHMENT

———◆·••◆———

My name, dear saint, is hateful to myself,
Because it is an enemy to thee.
— Shakespeare, "Romeo and Juliet"

Receiving the promised names from God involves first dealing with the old, defeating names given to us. Of course this is not very pleasant, but we can at least take heart that the joy of the new names awaits us. To begin, it is necessary to identify the leading phrases from which we have lived our lives and attempt to understand their origin and their power. The situation in ancient Judah during Isaiah's day provides a surprising number of insights for how we may begin this work.

Centuries ago, the people of God went through a terrible age when their names communicated hopelessness and despair. Before the collapse, however, there was a temple in Jerusalem. God's name dwelt there; it was a place where the omnipresent One was most especially present. At this temple, sacrifices were made and the promises of God were celebrated. But even in the days of splendor, not everyone could be described with joyful names.

Isaiah 56 mentions those who desired to participate fully in the worship of the Lord but were forbidden because they were not Hebrews by birth. They were aliens. The law expressly forbade their participation in the Passover celebration unless all the males in the family were circumcised (Exod. 12:43-48). And even then, some ethnic groups were to remain excluded for a number of generations (Deut. 23:3-8). Though drawn to the temple, these believers described themselves as "The LORD will surely separate me from his people" (Isa. 56:3). Their leading image, the name for the current state of their lives, was one of being shunned by God.

In the next verse, we read of the eunuchs, those men mutilated into sterility, either to serve a foreign queen or a pagan god. They were denied not only the hope of family and children but also the blessings of the Lord. Eunuchs were specifically forbidden from "the assembly of the LORD" (Deut. 23:1). The name these men took was, "I am just a dry tree" (Isa. 56:3).

Today in the United States, we find it hard to imagine an officially sanctioned exclusion of certain ethnic groups from worship. But we do not have to look far into our history to discover how we divided people by race, gender or class even in worship. Moreover, if we imaginatively consider the situations of the people forced to the outside in ancient Judah, and feel their feelings with them for a while, we realize that such alienation still exists in our churches. What happened to these people literally happens to us metaphorically. The foreigners and eunuchs of Isaiah 56 provide symbols—names—for the ways we are blocked from a free worship of God in open community with others.

BLOCKED FROM THE INNER CIRCLE

The alien feared, "The LORD will surely separate me." Many of us may feel as if God has excluded us from the inner circle of faith. We seem to be strangers to our own religion. On a Sunday morning, we look around and it appears as if everyone knows what is going on. People look as if they get it. But we may wonder how they manage. For we don't get it. We don't feel let in.

Do you ever wonder if there was some secret about religion that you weren't told? Did you miss the one Sunday school class where the keys to prayer were passed out? Some people never struggle for intimacy with God or comfort in worship. Others never feel at home. In this state, we may become church officers or ministers, hoping that this dedication will bring us closer to God. But it doesn't, and so many of us even as leaders are stumbling for direction.

It is not hard to feel like a stranger, even in your own home, in your own skin. We may feel as if we are always playing a game, one move ahead of being found out. Everyone seems to know the rules, but we worry that if questioned we will have to admit that we haven't got a clue. As long as the hands aren't called, we can keep playing. But there is a gnawing fear that we don't know what we are doing. We don't know how we survive at work, how to parent, how to live with others and alone.

Moreover, some people fear that they will always be misunderstood. Their perspective is not the same as the majority, and so they never quite fit anywhere. What they say seems to be misconstrued. They cannot communicate their feelings adequately and so they never feel heard. Every venture in communication risks the embarrassment of blank stares or feigned acknowledgement. They feel like foreigners in the world.

The doubly defeating experience of those aliens described in Isaiah 56 was that they had already "bound themselves" to God. They were living among the Israelites. They had given up their original gods for the Lord. Now their fate was tied up with the God of Israel, but they thought this God would exclude them from the assembly of worship and the sacred rituals.

Was this the experience of the Africans who were brought to America as slaves, given the story of Jesus by their captors, and yet never allowed to be full partners in the freedom of the gospel? Has this been the experience of many women who never felt the life and the work of the church was fully theirs? Unfortunately, nearly everyone who has spent any time in a church community has seen how God's people can mistreat those who do not fit the accepted profile of social standing and appearance. The tragedy, of course, is that when we are caught up in defining ourselves as in and others as outside the circle of favor, we can never feel quite accepted ourselves.

The category of foreigners in Isaiah 56 is not for those who have no connection to faith, but those who deal with God, who feel bound up with God yet cannot be comfortable. For any of us who relate to them, prayer then means approaching a God whom we're not sure wants to hear from us. Worship means entering a place where we don't feel that we fit. Striving to develop spiritually and serve meaningfully seems like a futile exercise. When we take the name "the LORD will surely exclude me," we know that spiritual diminishment is our lot.

THE NAME OF "DRY TREE"

Today we do not find many officially created eunuchs. Fortunately that has ceased to be a qualification for government service! Yet, there are many of us who feel what the eunuchs of Isaiah 56 felt: "I am just a dry tree." A couple longs for children and cannot have them. They wilt inside when they watch the families gambolling happily across the park. Some long to marry and never do. They do not understand how some people easily stumble into love while for all their care they cannot make a relationship last, nor turn the corner into intimacy. As the years pass, they feel joy drying up, and find they are turning an envious, mean eye toward others. Their boundaries narrow without others calling them forth. Life withers and they are trapped.

Others feel certain there is something they are to do with their lives, something they are to express, some way they are to help the world. But they are stymied. Their jobs do not call forth their spirits. The well begins to dry up: writer's block is not just for writers.

We may look back over our years and wonder why they have not been more fruitful. We have worked hard, tried our best in our relationships, served the church faithfully, yet seem to have nothing to show for it. We have made few lasting connections and our presence in the world seems to have made no real difference.

HOW DID WE BECOME THIS WAY?

How did we ever get to be such eunuchs? Some have been harmed so long ago that they scarcely remember it, but since that time, they have been dried up. On the most basic level, sexual abuse of a child can freeze the person all through adulthood. Just as effectively, a barrage of hurtful words through the years can cut off the soul from the waking, living person. Life is so hazardous that for protection the heart is sealed off. Their true life has withdrawn so deeply that it provides no nourishment for daily activity. The ensuing depression is the driest of dry trees. Gallons and gallons of water still don't reach its parched roots.

The world makes eunuchs of those who must make a living at jobs so repetitive and deadening that all creativity and capacity for joy is cut off. They work with no sight of the sky or sun. They are cut off from the green earth. And so there is often no spiritual impulse left except the longing for the oblivion of alcohol or hours of television.

Others have been sent onto paths of family expectation that proved impassable. They cannot measure up to the standard. Heritage proves overwhelming. But in the attempt to be what is expected, they have been cut off from their true path.

Many eunuchs in antiquity were created to be safe guardians of queens and princesses. They lost their hope for intimacy to serve the pleasure of the court. So people today have been harmed for the pleasure of the powerful and the many ways they exercise dominance. The mutilation of women in India or the practice of forced abortions in China are ghastly reminders that the powers in the world continue to turn fruitful vines into dry trees. Moreover, in less dramatic ways, many of us are struggling to bring forth life after the deadening effect of years of another's dominance.

But of course we are not only victims. We make ourselves spiritual eunuchs whenever we pursue a course of living that we want, but we know is not right for us. For instance, the heart may be cut off from the rest of us when we follow a prestigious marriage without love, just to keep our place in the world. Or, ministers get cut off from their calling if they follow the god of church growth and close their hearts to the poor. Many follow the path of striving to get the world's goods and the thrill of power, not knowing they are losing their souls until much later. Some essential spiritual life is blocked off when we pursue our sensual indulgences and never exercise any spiritual discipline. We all burn out when we run too hard without resting. When our inner and outer lives do not correspond, we dry up. Then we know well what it is to be, in George Herbert's phrase, simultaneously "rich and weary."

A NEW POSSIBILITY

Depressingly, then, it is not hard to identify with the alien who said, "The LORD will surely separate me" or the eunuch who said, "I am just a dry tree." These may be our inner names, the lead phrases out of which we live so that we never think we will know acceptance or fruitfulness again.

But Isaiah 56, does not only describe names of diminishment. Rather, God promises the eunuchs and the foreigners new names:

> To the eunuchs who keep my sabbaths,
> who choose the things that please me,
>   and hold fast my covenant,
> I will give, in my house and within my walls,
>   a monument and a name better than sons
>   and daughters;
>   I will give them an everlasting name
>   that shall not be cut off (56:4-5).

What could be better than children to a barren couple? God promises something which will come in the midst of their crushed state and still be better than the old, dashed, normal expectations. The mutilation will not be transformed magically, but fulfillment will be of another order.

The promise is of a name. The man who could father no children would have been concerned that his family name would be lost. Now comes the promise of an everlasting name within the temple of God. In God's house, in God's presence, the ones with no hope of a fruitful future will receive an everlasting legacy.

For us, this is the promise that life will count. It brings hope that love and life can be passed along to others in meaningful ways. God will view us not as mutilated but as whole and contributing. These verses anticipate Jesus' words, "Out of the believer's heart shall flow rivers of living water" (John 7:38). What seems dried up unto death shall become as fruitful as a well-watered garden.

It is pertinent that a Holocaust memorial in Jerusalem bears words from this passage in Hebrew: *yad vashem*, "a monument and a name" (Isa. 56:5). The memorial declares that meaning will come out of suffering. Those who were slaughtered will be recalled and valued continuously. So they will not be lost. Rather, they will become more than what was done to them. Though violence ended their physical lives on earth, the everlasting name from God has continued their presence among future generations.

A GREAT WELCOME

This chapter also includes a word of hope to those who feared they would be excluded from the company of God's people:

> And the foreigners who join themselves to the LORD,
> to minister to him, to love the name of the LORD,
> and to be his servants,
> all who keep the sabbath and do not profane it,
> and hold fast my covenant—

these I will bring to my holy mountain,
and make them joyful in my house of prayer;
their burnt offerings and their sacrifices
will be accepted on my altar;
for my house shall be called a house of prayer
for all peoples (56:6-7).

Here is a promise of being let in to intimacy with God. Our prayers will result in joy for they will be accepted. God will gather us in and not shut us out. We will be known fully and nevertheless loved completely. In Isaiah's vision, the ethnicity of the "foreigners" would not be changed, but rather welcomed. So our uniqueness will not be lost in a blending process, but rather celebrated. Our offerings, that which we have to contribute to God's glory, will be accepted. People will understand. Life will flow. What we do will have meaning. And so there will be a feeling of total inclusion. No longer will we feel like strangers but like those who have come to the spiritual home for which we have always longed.

The biblical scholar Alec Motyer has summarized the promise of this chapter:

> No-one is excluded from membership of God's people, either by nation or ancestry (the foreigner), accident of birth, parental or personal former affiliation to another god, falling below the creational standards of God or deep and fundamental personal defect (the eunuch). Middle walls of partition have come tumbling down between people and between people and the Lord.[1]

---

[1] J. Alec Motyer, *The Prophecy of Isaiah: An Introduction and Commentary* (Downer's Grove, IL: InterVarsity Press, 1993), 466.

In the promise of God, we will be welcomed, both by the Lord and the community of God's people. We will discover the fulfillment of the plan God has had all along: to extend his love out from the people of Israel to the entire world.

In this wonderful acceptance, we will find freedom from the names of diminishment that have burdened us for so long. We will be open to receive the new names which God has for us. But, of course, that entry into the assembly of the Lord still required that the welcomed people went on to follow through with worshipping the Lord with all their hearts, minds, and souls. In the same way, there is some essential work we must do to be able to claim the new names as our own. Isaiah 56 gives us clues for how we may begin that work and prepare for the new names. In the next chapter, then, we will consider how the foreigners and the eunuchs gained such access to the Lord's promises.

CHAPTER 2

LEAVING THE
OLD NAMES

———◦•◦•◦———

O, be some other name!
— Shakespeare, "Romeo and Juliet"

The aliens and the disfigured in Isaiah 56 were promised
that they could leave those diminishing descriptions behind.
We have hope that we too may become more than we have
been named by the world. Perhaps God's new names can
become part of our identity. But how do we receive these
names? How do we get in on these promises of joy and
acceptance? In this chapter, I'd like to lift out five of the
important activities which the Lord recognized as the way
the outcasts became part of the gathered people of God.
These may provide entry for us into the new names as well.

First, they joined themselves to the Lord (verses 3, 6).
The foreigners on Judah's soil willingly chose to align
themselves with the God of the Hebrews. They might have
been persuaded that at least paying lip service to the God of
the dominant people would have been convenient and
economically necessary. But this passage seems to be
describing a free acceptance that transcends the people of
the Lord and goes straight to a relationship with God.

Here was a radical empowerment of those who had
been excluded. God did not expect them to remain merely
victims. They had a choice. No matter how hopeless or bound

their lives might have appeared to be, their wills and souls remained their own. By consecrating their wills to God, they saw past those who would demean them or exclude them from full participation. With a higher vision than anyone would expect, they became bound to God.

This, perhaps, is analogous to the great faith of the African slaves who found the truth of the God who loved them in Jesus Christ even though their enslavers served the same God. They had no choice in where they lived or what they were made to do. But their spirits remained free to worship. Miraculously, they did not reject the God of their oppressors but found that God to be their true liberator. So, we too might see past the failings of people in the church and find welcome in Christ, the Lord of the church.

This is the hope that we can separate our understanding of God from harmful relationships in our families, from old ideas about the church, from damage done to us in the world, and see that God is beyond, deeper, more than all of those dominating voices. In an act of sheer trust, we go to God in the hope that we will be granted more grace than the world gives. We submit when we could stay justifiably enraged. We offer ourselves in service risking that God may be just another dominator. These foreigners who bound themselves to the Lord call us to open ourselves to life and God again even if terrible things have been done to us in the past. This is the call of the Spirit to life.

Second, they kept the sabbath (verses 4, 6). The sabbath was a day of rest ordained in the Ten Commandments and corresponded to God's rest after creating the world. It was a distinctive mark of the people of God. Keeping that day in holiness was a sign that one had responded to the offer of God who had said, "Now, therefore, if you obey my voice and keep my covenant, you shall be my treasured possession out of all the peoples" (Exod. 19:5). Ceasing from all work on the Sabbath was a deliberate act of not acting, and was so emphatic that God declared it "a sign between me and you throughout your generations" (Exod. 31:13).

In chapter 8, we will consider the role of the sabbath in receiving the new names from God more extensively. For now, we can begin by viewing sabbath observance as an intentional halt to trying to create our own lives, to justify our worth, and to be our own gods. Keeping the sabbath means recognizing that God is God. We order each week, and so our entire lives, around the worship of the Lord.

For one day in every seven, we cease doing all the striving which leads us to being cut off from ourselves and feeling like strangers in our own skin. Sabbath rest provides time for wounds to heal. It allows our roots to be watered and begin to sink down again into God. There is opportunity to worship on the sabbath and so we have a way to enter into God's rhythm for the world. The foreigners and the eunuchs were promised that keeping the sabbath was a way to enter a fruitful, joyful relationship with God. By stepping out of the world's rhythm, we too can shed the names this world throws on us the rest of the week. Entering God's time in sabbath rest, we are open to hearing his new names for us.

Third, they held fast to the covenant (verses 4-6). The covenant included more than the sabbath requirements. It represented the history of God's promises to the world and to a particular people. And it included the response God required from humanity. Holding fast to the covenant meant that the outcasts located themselves within the story of God's promises. While the dominant people might have easily ignored such strands of all-embracing love within their tradition, the aliens and eunuchs found and clung to the hope that God's love extended to them. When others were reading them out of the story, they had enough faith and tenacity to discover how God had invited them in to the covenant.

A brief look at the history of God's covenants can help us see that the work of God in the world has always had importance for all of humanity, even when God's primary focus was the people of Israel. From the beginning, God desired to bind himself to the people he had created. He offered the whole earth to humanity in creation, giving to Adam and Eve the care of the Garden, the naming of the animals, and the joy of one another. All that was asked in return was that the couple abstained from eating the fruit of one tree. This covenant of creation reveals the close relationship God has wanted with humankind, the creatures made in his image.

After the Flood, God made a new covenant not only with Noah, but with every creature on earth, promising constancy in the rhythm of the days and the seasons, and promising restraint from the divine wrath at humanity's sinfulness. From then on, God would bear in himself the pain of working with humankind, even though he knew "the inclination of the human heart is evil from youth" (Gen. 8:21). Compared to the capricious, punishing deities of the ancient Near East, Israel's stories of such long suffering constancy in a compassionate God would have been a compelling alternative for the foreign listeners.

Years later, God called Abram and Sarai out from their homeland to a place as vague as "the land that I will show you." In so doing, he promised Abram "I will make of you a great nation, and I will bless you, and make your name great, so that you will be a blessing . . . in you all the families of the earth shall be blessed" (Gen. 12:2-3). The plan was always that the people who lived in such a particular relationship to God would lead the rest of the world back to harmony with the Creator.

In the great covenant on Mount Sinai, God gave to Moses the Ten Commandments as a rule of life for the people God had specifically called as his own. Upon the mountain, the Lord told Moses, "Indeed, the whole earth is mine, but you shall be for me . . . a holy nation" (Exod. 19:5-6). God bound himself to the Hebrews and in return, they were to be obedient to the laws of the covenant. Thereby, Israel would lead the entire world to recognize the sovereignty of its loving, ordering God.

Centuries later, God made a covenant with David, promising that the shepherd king's heir "shall build a house for my name, and I will establish the throne of his kingdom forever" (2 Sam. 7:13). David's son Solomon indeed became king and had the temple built in Jerusalem, where God promised his name would dwell. During the dedication of the temple, Solomon understood that people from all over the world would be drawn to the presence of God in that place. He prayed:

> Likewise when a foreigner, who is not of your people Israel, comes from a distant land because of your name—for they shall hear of your great name, your mighty hand, and your outstretched arm—when a foreigner comes and prays toward this house, then hear in heaven your dwelling place, and do according to all the foreigner calls to you, so that all the peoples of the earth may know your name and fear you . . . .
>
> — 1 Kings 8:41-43

The point was always that the house of the Lord should be a house of prayer for all people. The distinctive presence of the Lord among a particularly chosen nation was meant to be a beacon of hope for the rest of the world.

The aliens and outcasts of Isaiah 56 held fast to the covenant that this all-embracing God had made with the world. Though the religious people might have forgotten the ultimate goal of gathering in everyone, the foreigners in Isaiah 56 held fast to the promises. They held to a higher vision of God than that of the religious insiders! They realized, more than the officially faithful, that the Lord is the Creator of all the earth and all people. His mercies not only endure forever but extend forever, to every place.

For us living under names of diminishment, this means rediscovering the covenants of God and learning how they were meant for us as much as anyone. Those who walk through their days bearing shining names of promise have little trouble believing that God's bounty is for them. But those of us who labor under heavy, defeating names may have to scrabble and claw to hold fast to the covenants. We have to learn from the scriptures that the promises are ours, and we hold on hard to them against the tearing winds of the world. God's authority makes them ours; the voices of diminishment do not have the final say.

The fourth way outcasts became part of the gathered people of God was they loved the name of the Lord (verse 6). Those formerly excluded would find that loving the name of the Lord led to receiving the everlasting name from God for themselves. So we learn that our names of diminishment can be changed by actively loving the name of God. In other words, when we focus on God's name, the leading phrases through which God expresses his heart, then we are transformed.

Towards the beginning of the story of Exodus, Moses asked for the name of the Lord and God replied, "I AM WHO I AM . . . Thus you shall say to the Israelites, 'I AM has sent me to you'" (Exod. 3:14). There is mystery in such a name, implying an unknowable greatness in God. From such a name, we glean that the Lord of Israel is the one who has always been and always will be. God is the creator and ruler of all. I AM also precedes and supersedes any powers which have tried to name us in diminishing ways. That God is our namer.

The outcasts, perhaps, would have been especially interested in the story of Hagar, the Egyptian slave-girl. When Abram and Sarai continued childless in spite of God's covenant promise, they decided to take matters into their own hands. Abram joined with Hagar and she soon conceived. Though Sarai had suggested the union, she could not bear the result and mistreated Hagar until she ran away. Hagar collapsed in the desert. Then an angel appeared to her, and gave her a comforting message from the Lord. She would indeed bear a son, and her offspring would multiply through the generations.

The result of this visitation in the desert was that Hagar learned the name of God through his promises. She was told to name the boy "Ishmael," which means "God hears." For God had heard her sorrow. And after the angel departed, Hagar "named the LORD who spoke to her, "You are El-roi," the God who sees (Gen. 16:13). God saw her desperate situation in the wilderness and had mercy upon her. The aliens who loved the name of the Lord adored the God who heard the cries of slave-girls and looked with compassion on the plight of foreigners.

Moreover, we read in 1 John that "God is love" (1 John 4:16). The truest name, the leading phrase which describes the essence of God, is love. The nature of such compassion is expressed in Isaiah 56 as God is self-described as one "who gathers the outcasts of Israel" (verse 8) and makes "them joyful in my house of prayer" (verse 7). The God of love is the great embracer of outcasts and the pourer of joy on those who come to him.

Loving a God with such a name lifts us out of ourselves to acknowledge God and all he desires to give us. And when we devote ourselves to the great I AM, the God who sees and loves, we find that God responds by renaming us, freeing us from the names of diminishment, and conferring instead titles of grace.

Last, they were given the command to say "No" to the names of diminishment (verse 3). Based on their devotion to the Lord through the activities we have considered, the foreigners and the eunuchs were instructed to refuse the titles of exclusion. God's acceptance of their love became the basis for thinking of themselves in new ways. They were now free to renounce what the voices within them and without them had told them for years. We read, "Do not let the foreigner joined to the LORD say . . . and do not let the eunuch say . . . (56:3)." God forbade them to speak of themselves with the old names!

Interestingly, the command can be taken two ways. The obvious way is instruction to the aliens and disfigured. They themselves are to change the way they speak. But we can also read the text as saying that the entire community of faith is to prevent them from living under the old names.

For God's own chosen people had perpetuated the excluded position of the foreigners in their midst. It had been too easy to look past the obvious devotion and the years of service and see only differences in ethnicity. God's people have historically been all too good at keeping "heathen" in their place. Now they were called to look beyond the ingrained habits of years. God beckoned them to see the larger vision which had always been present in the scriptures, though long neglected.

The outcasts do most of the work in rising above what others have named them to embrace the new names from God. The majority of people are too wrapped in their own concerns to be sufficient help. But nevertheless, the entire community of God's people is commanded to assist in the shedding of old names and the embracing of new ones. We have work to do in renaming the once excluded as those included now in God's covenant of grace.

So in this fifth activity, God encourages the diminished to lay aside the names of defeat. Based on the authority of God's revealed intent throughout history, they vault beyond the current practices to a brighter vision. And those of us who have begun living under names of grace are to help them. We come alongside and urge, "Say NO! to that name! You don't need it anymore. God has a new name for you."

This is more than mere positive thinking techniques. The shedding of the old names is based on God's call to the outcasts, and on the activity of those previously excluded ones to entrust themselves wholeheartedly to the Lord. It is a move beyond bitterness, no matter how justified that emotion may be by the circumstances of life. It is a move of faith that the God of love will prove to be steadfast and reliable in his grace.

Now we are ready to move into the next section, and to begin to consider the specific new names offered in the rest of Isaiah.

Part Two

———◦•◦•◦———

Receiving the Names
of our
Essential Identity

CHAPTER 3

THE VOICE THAT
CALLS IN THE NIGHT

◆━◆━◆

One of the ways we can receive the new names from God is to open ourselves through the use of imagination. Throughout this book, we hope to approach the new names through our hearts as well as our thoughts. At the beginning of each new section, then, you will find a brief story that has arisen from my own imagining about the new names in Isaiah. The following story is meant to lead you more deeply into the feelings associated with the names of diminishment in Isaiah 56 and then to experience the wonderful turn toward the names of promise found in Isaiah 62. I invite you to read it as a prelude to the succeeding chapters, and then to return to it again after you have considered the new names of our essential identity.

> In the morning of your life, you went out to the fields and began to plant. The work was hard but the soil was good and the sun was kind. You planted for a rich harvest. In one corner of your land you worked on a vineyard. You made the arbor for the young grape vines to climb. In another section you plowed the ground and planted wheat. You gave thanks to God for the strength to work, for the earth and the seed, for the hope of the harvest.
>
> In the fullness of time, you were sure a rich

crop would be produced. Soon, as a reward for your labors, grapes on the vine would be pressed and turned to wine. Wheat would be gleaned and cracked and baked into bread. Bread and wine, the staff and cup of life. You imagined how you would take your place among the other landowners, talking over the finer points of the season's weather and the state of the fields. You could hear the hearty laughter of such comraderie.

You imagined that one day you would have a place in the community. No longer would you be striving to earn your place, but it would have been gained. You would speak and others would listen. They would understand what you said, value your thoughts, and reply. You would carry your share in the life of the community and be respected. You would be known.

And there would be a family with many children. A spouse who adored you would become your partner. Babies who reached their arms to you would quickly be transforming into handsome young men and women, ready as you were now to enter the world.

Yes, in the morning of your life, this was your dream and your expectation. It seemed almost to be true. In your imagination, you could hear the sounds of fulfillment: the laughter of children, wind dancing through the wheat the fields, your spouse singing love through the home.

Now it is late in the morning, and you have left your land and your home, and your dreams, just for a while. You need to go to town for supplies. There is lightness in your step as you walk toward the store where your parents once bought their tools for farming, their food for meals, the hardware and furnishings for their homes.

With hope, you reach the store and enter, expecting a greeting. Instantly you feel that something is wrong. The atmosphere is thick with tension. You feel as if you have walked into a private conversation without invitation. You are not welcome here.

Hard eyes look at you with no glimmer of recognition. You try as best you can to be jovial in your greeting. They seem insulted that you have called them by name.

A woman quickly rolls up the brightly colored fabrics she had spread on a table. You will not have a glimpse of such finery. A man closes the lid on a box full of new farming tools. These are not for sale. The sack of grain is drawn tight. A curtain is pulled over the shelves of food.

Still, you know these people, this store, this town. You ask for what you need. Maybe this is all a joke. These good people wouldn't treat you this way. But they do. "Your money is no good here. We don't sell to foreigners."

"Foreigner?" you plead. "I'm no stranger to you folks. You've known me since I was a baby. Come on, let me buy what I need so my crops can grow and my land prosper."

But there is no reply, except a harsh voice which says, "We're closed. Be on your way."

You back out of the door into the streets. No one will look you in the eye. They look past you, except for the children who point and whisper. You go to another shop. The sign reads, "Closed."

"Let me in!" you cry. But there is no reply except silence.

You will not be let in. You are not known. You are a stranger in your own town. An alien.

You begin to walk home. And the friendly sun of your life's morning has become an early afternoon blaze. Your skin is burning and your clothes are stained with sweat. Old friends pass by but no one offers you a ride. The way to your home seems to take years.

When you finally reach your fields, you cannot believe your eyes. You had just been here this morning, but they look as if no one has tended them in decades. The grapevines have grown wild over the arbor. Unpruned for all this time, the grapes on the vine are few. And they are sour. The arbor is now a shelter for snakes and desert lizards.

Out in the wheat fields, the land is parched. Desolate. The grain is crisping in the sun, good only as tinder for the wildfires which could ride in on this heat. It hasn't rained.

You run into the house. Where is spouse you dreamed you had? Where are the children? It is empty. There is no trace that you were ever anything but alone.

Your morning dreams of fertile fields and waving rows of wheat have become visions of drought. The hope of a place in the community has evaporated. You are a stranger here. And there will be no fruit of the womb or seed of the loins. You might as well be a eunuch.

You sit down in despair. And do not even hear

the soldier who comes upon you. He prods you with the point of a spear. "Who are you and what are you doing trespassing on the king's lands?"

"I own this land," you say, "This is my house."

"You own nothing. Your house will be the king's brickyards. Come with me."

And so it is that you are dragged far from your land. Nothing feels like home anymore. You are put to work, but the work is not fulfilling; it is not what you had planned at all. In the afternoon of your life, you spend your strength laboring from sunrise to sunset to make bricks for a king who is not your king in a land that is not your land, among people who do not know you. You work and you are not rewarded. You talk and no one hears. One day is the same as the next. Endless toil to no end.

With every day that passes, hope is harder to find. You cannot remember being anything else. You are forsaken. Your name might as well be "Desolate." Your hometown is called, "Deserted."

At night, on your mat, you are exhausted. Though the flies buzz around your head and the heat bakes in the roof above you, you fall into thick, beaten sleep. One night, a breeze nibbles away at the heat. Still dosing, you hear a sound you have not heard in years. You hear someone singing. Very softly. Carried on the thinnest night breeze, the words reach you in sleep, "My delight is in her. That is your name. Hephzibah: My Delight. They will call you Hephzibah because they will see how I delight in you."

The next morning when you wake, you shake your head for the strangeness of the dream. It brought the sweetest feeling you have had in months. But quickly it is forgotten through the demands of the day. It was, after all, only a dream.

That night, you think of it again. You look at your hands. They are rough from work. The nails are cracked and caked with dirt. Your fingertips are swollen. Cuts on your hands seem never to get cleaned. Some are infected; there are scars.

You feel your hair and it is matted with dirt. Even to your dull fingers, the wrinkles and cracks on your face can be found. Your mouth hurts with toothache. Your muscles are thinning and your back is in spasm. In spite of it all, a dry chuckle comes forth. You are remembering the fantasy you had of a wedding, and a home and children. "I'd be quite the desirable partner now! Who would ever have me if I did get free of here?" The humor is quickly lost, however, as you realize how quickly your shining morning has passed through bleak afternoon toward a dreary evening. Sleep finally takes you away.

But again the song comes in the night. "Hephzibah, My Delight, your land shall again be yours, and all who see it will call it Beulah: Married. For your children, and there will be many children, will marry your land and cause it to break forth in rich harvest. You will be called Sought After, for I will desire you all your days."

The next morning, the hope does not fade with your toil, but persists through the day. Now night after night, the song of the Voice comes to you. It is calling you forth from the disappointment your life has been. In the midst of forsakenness, someone is seeking you. In the midst of being an exile and an alien, someone is letting you in. In the midst of dashed dreams and a harvest of thorns, someone is promising that your land will blossom with fruit.

And you begin to say, amidst your daily toil, "My name is Hephzibah, My Delight." And into the bleakness of your cell you breathe the song, "The land of my life is Beulah, Married and adored. My name is Sought After."

And it seems to be the morning of your life again.

CHAPTER 4

SOUGHT OUT

———— •◦••◦• ————

Jesus sought me when a stranger, wandering from the fold of God.

> — Robert Robinson, "Come, Thou Fount
> of Every Blessing"

In the worst of times, God promised the people new names and a bright future. These names are still available to us. They speak to the very essence of how we think of ourselves. They carry into our depths God's great love. But before we receive them, we will walk in the darkness just a little while longer. For to know the joy of just how far God searches to bring us home, we have to consider for a moment more the extent of our exile.

A deserted town is an eerie place to walk. The streets, built for traffic, are too quiet. Windows, which sparkled years ago with glass, are boarded up with cheap wood. The last stores hold on precariously as their customers dwindle away. Their wares are musty. The owners remember the Saturdays when the sidewalks teemed with people.

Down the cracking street a building long unused has collapsed on itself. Once an architect designed it with an eye toward a different future than this one. Builders made it to last with the proper care now long withdrawn. A brisk commerce used to go on inside those walls. Now it is a home for rodents and birds who gather the yellowed papers from the floor to be used for their nests. Once those sheets signalled important business.

Hardly anyone goes through town anymore. The highways bypass it, and the shoppers head for banks, movies, and stores that have more sparkle and warmth to draw them. This is not what the town council envisioned a century ago.

The desertion was worse than that, however, in Jerusalem in the time of the exile in 587 B.C. The proud, strong walls which had withstood invaders for years were pulled down. The temple was desecrated as the conquerors violated the house of God, stealing its treasures and setting it ablaze. Only a burned out shell remained. The Babylonians reduced the city to rubble and carted off the citizens to their country far to the north.

We begin our study of the names of our essential identity by considering the worst of names. For in promising a new future, Isaiah also named the desolation: "You shall no more be termed *Forsaken,* and your land shall no more be termed *Desolate*" (62:4, italics mine).

During the exile, not just the foreigners and the eunuchs, but the entire country of Judah, and especially the holy city of Jerusalem suffered. The nation fell under God's judgment for rebelliousness, and Isaiah envisioned the forsakenness of a people taken in what has become known as the Babylonian Captivity. In chapter 64, the people prayed, "Your holy cities have become a wilderness. . . . Our holy and beautiful house, where our ancestors praised you, has been burned by fire, and all our pleasant places have become ruins" (verses 10-11).

There are millions of refugees today whose souls would

resonate with these passages. Adrift on the high seas in flimsy boats, or waiting behind the fences of detention centers, they know the meaning of the word "forsaken." Their homelands have been destroyed by civil war, natural disaster or famine. Places once holy, once nurturing, have been desecrated. How desolate must their cities have become to inspire setting out for such exile?

EXILE

Metaphorically, many of us in far safer environments also experience exile. A great many of us take stock of our lives and consider that we are not doing what we thought we would be doing. We are not where we wanted to be, and we do not know how to get home from the foreign life in which we find ourselves. We feel lost because "all our pleasant places have become ruins." Life wasn't supposed to be this way.

For instance, who anticipates the exile often associated with old age? Our elderly, once vigorous, may wander antiseptic halls in search of their right minds. They ask strangers to take them home. Not sure where they are, they know enough that this place of sharp scents and intermittent wails from other rooms is not their own land. This is a terrifying desolation both to witness and to consider as the future which may await us.

Who gets married anticipating the desert of divorce? A woman once dreamed of a lifelong partnership, while rearing a family amidst increasing prosperity. Instead, she now struggles to maintain her children in the home which is familiar to them but now far too costly. She is too exhausted even to rest well for the few hours she has to sleep, and can't remember the last time she was touched with affection. She is forsaken. This was not in her mind on the clear sunny afternoon of her wedding.

Who begins a career anticipating being stuck in a monotonous job for years, afraid to make a change, blocked from advancement, and quickly aging out of new possibilities? Yet a man who had boyhood dreams of brilliant success and exciting work may realize that his labor is little more than keeping up with an endless treadmill. Anyone may feel this way. Those who realize that the kitchen will never be clean feel the same desolation as the physicians who despair that the waiting room will never be empty. A plush office can be a more secure prison than an assembly line. We may find ourselves exiled from the land of rest, creativity, and meaningful accomplishment.

Did the young actor living robustly with a wide circle of friends ever anticipate a stroke in his thirties? The pleasure of drinking in the land of companionship became the struggle with addiction in his exile. He could no longer work, even as a short order chef. He became dependent and most of his friends vanished. Now he has to ask for help with everything. And he feels unwanted. A spirit of desolation rings his soul, and whispers that he is good for nothing. How long has it been since someone wanted him just for himself?

For so many of us, the present situation is not how life was going to be. We did not anticipate working so hard for so little return. We did not expect to be so lonely this far along. As the Beatles sang in the song "Golden Slumbers," "Once there was a way to get back home." But now such a path seems lost. We are cut off from vital life, intimacy and wholeness. We are, in Isaiah's metaphor, a city that is forsaken. There is very little traffic or commerce. No one comes into town and so we feel that we are not desirable. We are avoided and discarded. Our thoughts are desolate. The windows of our hearts are boarded up, the streets of our souls broken and empty. We merely exist.

SOUGHT OUT

The hope in the new names from God is that though we may feel utterly lost, we have not been abandoned. No matter how far the town of our life seems to have fallen off the map, God seeks to renew us. God has for us a better place. This exile does not have the last word. God desires to bring us, to bring the whole world, home to a joy and a glory we have scarcely imagined. To those in captivity, who feel lost and "unhomed," the word comes from God, "I am looking for you. I am seeking you. I know how to get you back home."

So it was that at the uttermost reaches of their exile in Babylon, a new name came to God's people on the winds of the Spirit: ". . . you shall be called Sought Out, A City Not Forsaken" (62:12). This was the thin thread of promise which tethered the people to a future that would lead them home. They were not forgotten. God would find his ruined children and bring them back to Jerusalem. They would rebuild the city, more glorious than before. They would restore the land to fertility and their children would flourish. Life would be renewed.

The word of the Lord to all of us in any form of exile is, "You shall be called Sought Out." Those who believe they are far from the life they envisioned may hear the news that someone is looking for them. Lostness is not our permanent state. Loneliness will be filled with the arrival of the One who seeks us.

GOD'S HUMILIATION

Throughout the Old Testament, "seeking" generally refers to the ways people turn their attention toward God. Seeking God is an orientation of the heart towards the One whom we believe is there, though unseen. We pray; we follow the commands; we worship; we look after others; we remember that God is the source of our lives. This is a need built into the very heart of us. We are prone to wander, however, and the scriptures continually point to seeking God as the way home. Psalm 105:4 rallies us to "Seek the LORD and his strength; seek his presence continually." And Isaiah 55:6 contains the instructions, "Seek the LORD while he may be found, call upon him while he is near." Throughout the Bible, God's people are called to return to the Creator by this spiritual activity of seeking.

The idea that God seeks us was introduced late in Israel's history. Before Isaiah, the only place I found a reference to God as the seeker was in Psalm 119. The psalmist prayed, "I have gone astray like a lost sheep; seek out your servant" (Psalm 119:176). The answer to this prayer for God to seek the lost was realized in the time of the exile as one of the divine attributes of God's love. Ezekiel, another prophet of the time, picked up the metaphor of God as the shepherd: "I myself will search for my sheep, and will seek them out. I will seek the lost, and I will bring back the strayed, and I will bind up the injured, and I will strengthen the weak . . ." (Ezek. 34:11, 16).

There is a measure of humility implied by such seeking. If we are indifferent to the situation of others, we do not seek out their company. If people have nothing that we want or need, we do not pursue them. So, in seeking the people, God reveals that he desires them not only in altruistic love, but because in some way they affect him. That is an amazing realization to have in the midst of exile, feeling unlovely and unnecessary. And it is deeply satisfying. I do not want simply to be someone's charity project, no matter how much I may need that charity. I want to be sought because finding me will give benefit to the seeker. God wants us, even as we are, and so he seeks us. Something in us is desirable to him, no matter how marred our lives have been. Given the name Sought Out, we have value. We have something God wants. This gives us an intrinsic attractiveness beyond merit or situation.

And so God is vulnerable to our response. In Isaiah 65:1 God spoke, "I was ready to be sought out by those who did not ask, to be found by those who did not seek me. I said, 'Here I am, here I am,' to a nation that did not call on my name." Here is the image of God with outstretched arms, waiting while his children spurn him and the watching universe laughs. It is a picture of a parent aching for the crying child to be enfolded in loving arms. But the child scampers away and remains miserable.

Isaiah brought us the early glimpses of the heart of God that seeks after the lost, no matter how broken they have been by the hand of others, no matter their indifference to God or even how much they deserve to be in exile. In the New Testament, the curtain is pulled back further, and we see clearly revealed in Jesus this essential seeking quality of God.

Jesus said in Luke after calling the tax collector Zacchaeus, "For the Son of Man came to seek out and to save the lost" (Luke 19:10). Jesus came to bring us home from exile. He came to find us when we thought we were forsaken, and restore us to a flourishing life. In the parable of the lost sheep, Jesus compared God to a shepherd who will leave ninety sheep exposed in the wilderness while he goes off to seek one that is lost. "When he has found it, he lays it on his shoulders and rejoices" (Luke 15:5). God's seeking love knows no bounds.

Then in John 10, Jesus identified himself with the good shepherd and brought in the activity of naming which goes with seeking. He said, "He calls his own sheep by name and leads them out. I am the good shepherd. The good shepherd lays down his life for the sheep. My sheep hear my voice. I know them, and they follow me. I give them eternal life, and they will never perish. No one will snatch them out of my hand" (John 10:3, 11, 27-28).

The tenderness of this shepherding, seeking love is evoked in Henry Williams Baker's famous hymn "The King of Love My Shepherd Is." He writes:

> Perverse and foolish, oft I strayed,
> But yet in love he sought me;
> And on his shoulder gently laid,
> And home, rejoicing, brought me.

The news that we are sought ends the fear that we are abandoned and the worry that God's anger will strike us. When we know ourselves as sought and found, we learn the comfort of riding home on the shepherd's shoulders. We feel the joy God has in being with us.

A MEMORY

It is frightening to be lost, in the woods for a few hours, in the wilderness for days, or in an alien country for a season. Despair can set in if we become convinced that no one knows, or cares, where we are. If no one is looking for us, our lostness seems permanent. But in even the most dire circumstances, hope can persist if we believe that rescuers are searching.

I can remember going to a boat show with my father as a young child. There was a huge crowd of people looking at all the displays. I remember turning around and seeing what I thought was my father's pants leg. I walked over and grabbed the trousers. But when I looked up to the face attached to those pants, I saw only a stranger. The whole world changed. I didn't know what to do. The room seemed so much bigger than it had only a moment ago. I was lost.

Then I heard my name called, and my father came out of the crowd to take my hand. He hadn't forgotten me for a second. He was seeking me as soon as we were separated. What seemed like hours of lostness to me was actually less than a minute. I felt such relief at being found. I had not realized before how contented I was to be with my father in that large convention center. It was his presence, in fact, that made the difference between a dangerous, disconcerting hour and an afternoon of shared adventure and excitement.

The hope in the name Sought Out is that we are never separated from the providential care and love of God. We are not ever completely lost because God always knows where we are. Our Lord is always looking for us, always calling us home.

Such a promise came to the exiles of Judah before it was a reality. The people who received the vision were still in captivity. And so they were given a hope to which they clung while they waited for God's word to be fulfilled. They took the names as a guarantee of what would come to be, though it might take years to realize.

So we too may hear God's words to us before our present experience of lostness has been changed. The new name is the call of hope which leads us home. Can you feel God seeking you? Can you hear the Lord calling? I hear God's voice like this:

"I have not abandoned you. Though your good health may have forsaken you, I have not. Those whom you love may have left you, but I did not. Your plans may have been thwarted, your vision marred, your dreams dashed. But I am still here, and I have a vision for your life greater than you can yet imagine. Your faith may have left you, but I have not. Your belief in me may have withered, but my love for you still flourishes. I am seeking you, calling you by name. You are desirable to me. I want you to be with me. Your presence matters to me; your life affects mine. I am seeking you because I want you. You are as precious to me as my own life. You are Sought Out."

CHAPTER 5

THE REDEEMED
OF THE LORD

＊

*See, I have inscribed you on the palms
of my hands.*

— Isaiah 49:16

As wonderful as it is to be named Sought Out, we know that
it is not enough. For even in our desolation, there is something in many of us that desires to stay lost and exiled. We
do not want to be found. We are afraid that God will judge
us. Our secret shames will come to light, and we will be
found wanting for all we have done and even for what has
been done to us.

Moreover, we may fear the loss of our independence
and would rather be miserable and free (supposedly) than
safe but kept in the Shepherd's fold. If we go home to God,
we suspect that some of our favorite habits will have to be
let go. For our ways of coping with the harshness of the
world may have been destructive, or, dare we say it, sinful.
We know those will have to change. And so, though our
souls ache to be found, we hide among the ruins.

We may experience a certain amount of pressure in
being named Sought Out. There arises an internal awareness
that God is waiting for us to notice. And it makes us
nervous. Often we run from this pressure of being sought.
We mistakenly think that what God wants is the very

opposite of what we want. In fact, we may think that God, and what has been done in his name, has been part of our suffering all along. We worry that God is anxious to drag us from what is familiar into difficult "religious" service.

When a friend of mine lived in a tiny apartment in New York City, I had to share the living room with his yellow labrador during my visits. In the morning, the dog would sit next to the hide-a-bed, watching me sleep. I could feel his breath. If I so much as opened one eye, he'd be all over me, demanding, all at once, a walk, a pat, a bowl of food, and a round of tug-o-war. Many of us have experienced the seeking of God as this kind of vigil over us. We think that if we open ourselves even for a second, God will demand something from us. And we feel sure it will be more disturbing than leaving a warm bed to take out a dog at freezing dawn. So we may try to stay still under the covers as long as possible, eyes shut to the One who watches.

And for a while, God does not pull back the blankets. For, in seeking us, God has given us the power of refusal. Even the weakest of us may stubbornly exercise that right. We may hide. And then, when the presence of God seems to us a relentless insistence, we run from it. In an infinite variety of ways, we may flee God. Francis Thompson understood this impulse and the canine tenacity of our seeking God when he composed "The Hound of Heaven." In it, he wrote:

> I fled Him, down the nights and down the days;
>   I fled Him, down the arches of the years;
> I fled Him, down the labyrinthine ways
>   Of my own mind; and in the midst of tears
> I hid from Him . . .

Up vistaed hopes I sped . . .
. . . .
From those strong feet that followed, followed after.
    But with unhurrying chase,
    · And unperturbéd pace,
Deliberate speed, majestic instancy
    They beat—and a voice beat
    More instant than the feet—
"All things betray thee, who betrayest Me."

We flee, but God pursues. While we are on the lam, we think we are free. But all the while life is unravelling. Here is the real problem in all our running. When we refuse to be found by our Creator, we are in exile from who we were made to be. We strive to make a home in a foreign land, and it never quite works. But the longer we stay away, the less memory of our true homeland we have. The longer we run, the greater the chaos grows. And when humanity collectively refuses God, this disharmony breeds distorted relationships, injustice, and ultimately violence. All things betray us, as Thompson wrote, when we have betrayed our God.

JUDAH'S REFUSAL

The people of God in Isaiah's day suffered at the hands of foreign invaders. It must have seemed terribly unjust to an average family as they were dragged away from the homes they loved. How could a loving God be so wrathful? Of course there was no excuse for the violence of the Babylonians. The individual citizen of Jerusalem did not cause the lust of conquest nor offer flame for the torching of the temple.

But from a broader perspective, we know that the seeds

of this downfall were planted long before. And each individual contributed to the collective decline of the nation. Already the kingdom had been sundered by civil strife in 930 B.C. King David's great nation became the northern kingdom of Israel and the southern kingdom called Judah, where Jerusalem was. Isaiah was one of many prophets who warned the people through the years that they were failing to love God with their whole, undivided hearts.

They had settled in a multicultural region, and there were many other gods competing for attention. These idols were of a manageable size; statues of them could be found adorning the finest homes; they made more sense to the everyday citizen. And so the people played both sides of the religious fence. Moreover, the prosperity of the kingdom had led quite easily to the excesses of greed and sensuality we know so well today. The less they were tethered to their God, the easier it was for them to let matters of truth and justice to be corrupted.

The society had been disintegrating well before the exile. Isaiah and his people of Judah witnessed the fall of Israel in the north in 722, so they had a clear example of where the path of unfaithfulness could lead. But they continued to grow internally weak. The result was a sense of national dismay. Isaiah described it:

> . . . we wait for light, and lo! there is darkness . . .
> we stumble at noon as in the twilight . . . We all
> growl like bears; like doves we moan mournfully. We
> wait for justice, but there is none; for salvation but it
> is far from us. For our transgressions before you are
> many, and our sins testify against us (59:9-12).

Then, with poetic brilliance, Isaiah summarized the decline by personifying the virtues that had been driven from daily life in the city:

> Justice is turned back, and righteousness stands at a distance; for truth stumbles in the public square, and uprightness cannot enter. Truth is lacking, and whoever turns from evil is despoiled (59:14-15).

The image was that of a nation in which concern for telling the truth was no longer part of public discussions. Religion became a hollow form. Issues of justice were held back from business dealings. Those who swam against the tide of greed were scorned. The culture attempted to expel both God and virtue. They did not want to be found. And so, the society was collapsing in upon itself. They fairly invited the exile.

In the same way, our attempts to live without God lead to collapse, whether as individuals or communities. Justice is driven out as part of our freedom to pursue our own ends. Truth gets a quick nudge in the potholed streets so our deceptions need not come to light. We identify God with the source of the sufferings we have undergone and thereby cut ourselves off from the source of healing. All God's seeking of us can feel like just so much more oppression. So we may get caught in a wrenching paradox whereby we simultaneously long to be found and to stay lost. Our own fears, as well as our willfulness, keep us from hearing our new names.

REDEMPTION

God understood that the people had gone so far down the road that they could not turn around without assistance. The spirit of the age had them too strongly in its grip. The help

God provided included allowing the foretold consequences
of their rebellion. He stopped saving them from their
choices for a while so that he could save them more fully in
the future, after they understood where their flight led. God
declared the exile to be divine wrath, evoked by the
outworking of human free will. But God was not content to
let things remain that way. Isaiah continued:

> The LORD saw it, and it displeased him that there was
> no justice. He saw that there was no one,
> and was appalled that there was no one to intervene;
> so his own arm brought him victory,
> and his righteousness upheld him.
> And he will come to Zion as Redeemer,
> to those in Jacob who turn from
>   transgression (59:15-16, 20).

God did what the people could not do for themselves.
This can be a hard reality to accept. Alone, we cannot find
our way back from exile nor repair the ruins either of our
individual lives or our culture. We do not even want to. We
need an act of God. Such a freeing deliverance is known as
redemption. God promised through Isaiah that he would
come himself to enact this salvation. The Lord would arrive
as the Redeemer and recreate his people.

This leads to the second of our new names: "They shall
be called the Holy People, the Redeemed of the LORD"
(62:12).

These acts of the Redeemer, however, did not occur all
at once. There were stages to the way Isaiah's prophecy
unfolded. After the captivity, which was a promised
consequence for the sins of Judah, there would come by the
work of the Redeemer:

1) the return from exile, which brought judgement on the captors and deliverance to the captives;

2) the spiritual redemption of God's people whereby faithfulness and justice would be reborn in the nation;

. 3) the worldwide gathering to a Jerusalem illumined by the presence of God.

The first part of the redemption of the people of Judah began with their release from captivity forty-eight years later. The promised Redeemer appeared to be Cyrus of Persia. When the Persians conquered the Babylonians, the world stage changed. And the new ruler became a friend of the Hebrews. He let them go home. The first stage seemed swiftly accomplished.

But the return from exile was not a full redemption. It became clear quickly that the prophecies of Isaiah were about more than a move back home. The promised Redeemer had to be more than a benevolent foreign ruler. He was identified with the coming of the Lord himself. He was the one who would make a broken and rebellious nation into the Holy People. And that did not happen simply with the return to Jerusalem. Isaiah looked beyond the immediate years to a future restoration of Israel from the inside out. This second stage of redemption would have to be accomplished by the Messiah, the Anointed One, who was God come among us.

Christians understand these passages in light of our faith that Jesus of Nazareth was indeed the promised Redeemer. Isaiah 61 begins with the words Jesus read in his first recorded sermon in Luke 4:

> The spirit of the Lord God is upon me,
> because the LORD has anointed me;

he has sent me to bring good news to the oppressed,
to bind up the brokenhearted,
to proclaim liberty to the captives,
and release to the prisoners (61:1).

After reading this passage in the synagogue, Jesus declared, "Today this scripture has been fulfilled in your hearing" (Luke 4:21). The work of the Anointed Redeemer is Jesus' work. In his life, death and resurrection, Jesus did what we cannot do for ourselves. He secured forgiveness and broke the power of sin and death. He is able now to grant us the power to be restored from the damage that has been done to us and to be freed from the willfulness that arises from within. His love relieves the fear that keeps us on the run. In Jesus the second stage of Isaiah's prophecy has been fulfilled.

But the third stage, that of the worldwide gathering to Jerusalem, still awaits fulfillment. We understand the redemption brought by Jesus is for the entire waiting world. The hope extends through and beyond Judah now to all people. The vision, though, has not yet been fully realized. The new heavens and the new earth promised in Isaiah 66:22 are promised again at the end of the New Testament in Revelation 21. The days when all tears have been wiped away, and sorrow and dying are no more remain ahead. The Redeemer has work yet to do.

THE SHEPHERD WHO CASTS OUT FEAR

Isaiah's vision of the Redeemer brings us the hope that God will not allow the world to continue the way it is, but will come to end injustice, even though the world will have to be wrenched back into alignment and jolted back into truth. It is bad news for the part of us that wants to stay hidden, for all will be found out and brought to light. But it is tremendously good news for the part of us that admits brokenness and desires to be healed.

Returning to our image of the seeking Shepherd, we can see in John 10 how the Shepherd's work is a sacrificial care of the sheep which secures for them more life than they could ever have on their own. Jesus said:

> I came that they might have life, and have it abundantly. I am the good shepherd. I know my own and my own know me, just as the Father knows me and I know the Father. And I lay down my life for the sheep. My sheep hear my voice. I know them, and they follow me. I give them eternal life, and they will never perish. No one will snatch them out of my hand.
>
> —John 10:10, 14, 27-28

The Redeemer came not to shame us or make us something other than what we were created to be. He came to give us abundant, eternal life, the life of the everliving God flowing from within us both in the present and beyond death in the world to come. He was willing to go as far as to lay down his life for the sheep for their protection and for their future. They are held safely, securely, within his loving hand forever.

Later in the New Testament, John reflected further on this love when he wrote:

> . . . God is love. God's love was revealed among us in this way: God sent his only Son into the world so that we might live through him. In this is love, not

that we loved God but that he loved us and sent his
Son to be the atoning sacrifice for our sins. There is
no fear in love, but perfect love casts out fear."
—1 John 4:8-10, 18

There is nothing to fear from the One who names us
Sought Out. He seeks us in order to bring life to the places
deadened by shame. We slowly pull down the covers and
open an eye to see the face of the One who comes not to
condemn but to forgive. He names us Redeemed, those
bought back from futility. He pays the debts owed to our
inner tormentors so we can hear his voice instead of their
accusations. He brings us home from life on the run. The
Redeemer gives us his own name in calling us the
Redeemed. We are the recipients of his loving work. He
calls us the Holy People because the Holy One has named
us as his own. There is nothing to fear in receiving the
new names.

So we discover that God's seeking is the pressure from
within for us to be most fully and truly who we were created
to be, and it is the call to lift our sight beyond ourselves to
the Creator who made us and yearns for us every moment.

Of course there are changes which follow receiving
such a name. Life at home is very different than exile. It
takes a while to learn to stop using the survival tactics from
the days of captivity. We will fear dropping our facade of
independence. We will be tempted to run from revealing the
soft parts of our hearts. It will seem foolish to share our
brokenness with others. We might even be embarrassed
among our contemporaries that we're going by such a
"spiritual" name now. But love casts out fear. The Shepherd
will care for the needs of the sheep.

RECEIVING THE NAMES

Yes, we run from God. Even when we know better, we may still flee. But ultimately there is no place where we can safely hide. The Hound of Heaven is on our heels. The Good Shepherd knows the land better than the sheep, and he always finds us. He does what we cannot do. He redeems us from our participation in the world's resistance and all the consequences which follow. Jesus offers eternal life: life that is abundant and overflowing now, no matter the circumstances, and life that endures to everlasting ages in the future.

Robert Robinson's well known hymn from 1758, "Come, Thou Fount of Every Blessing," contains a prayer to help us cease hiding and receive the names Sought Out, the Holy People, the Redeemed of the Lord.

> Jesus sought me when a stranger,
> Wandering from the fold of God;
> He, to rescue me from danger,
> Interposed his precious blood.
>
> O to grace how great a debtor
> Daily I'm constrained to be!
> Let thy goodness like a fetter,
> Bind my wandering heart to Thee.
>
> Prone to wander, Lord I feel it,
> Prone to leave the God I love;
> Here's my heart, O take and seal it,
> Seal it for thy courts above.

God seeks you, and he has redeemed you in Christ, already. You may take the name by deciding to be found. Let the name that implies all God has done for us from the promise of Isaiah to the work of Jesus Christ be yours. You will be called the Redeemed of the Lord, a Holy People, because God calls you apart to be one of his own. He calls you, and his sheep know his voice.

CHAPTER 6

MY DELIGHT
IS IN HER

——◆•◆•◆——

*I have loved you with an everlasting
love . . .*
— Jeremiah 31:3

Over a deep gorge a hawk catches a thermal and rides the air upwards without ever beating its wings. "Watch me!" cries a boy as he skates along a street as fast as he can. A purple crocus opens its colors to the world in defiance of the winter that still grips the earth. A dog races through the woods as if on a level plain, nimbly leaping rocks and navigating around trees. She moves like wind. Spring sunlight coaxes out the deep red in my beloved's hair.

These things bring me delight. For a moment I am outside myself, taking pleasure in someone else. There is joy in the sight of another's being. Such moments collapse quickly into the pool of my usual considerations about what all this has to do with me, the supposed center of the universe. But they are enough to teach me what it is to delight in something for its own sake, in thankfulness for its existence. I feel happiness on behalf of the other.

Can it be that God takes such pleasure in us? In making us, the one who "fills all in all" withdrew enough of himself to give us a life in which he could delight. We have been given real choices and an open future. We were made with the potential for pleasing God so that his pleasure in us could be increased. And we were created to find our deepest joy in a reciprocal delight in God. And from the beginning that was so. When he had finished creating us male and female in his image, "God saw everything that he had made, and indeed, it was very good" (Gen. 1:31).

Of course, we know that the image of God was marred in the Garden by the willful choices of the man and the woman. The story of the Bible is the story of God's attempts to draw us back to himself, to restore the divine imprint within us. It is a long, twisting tale, full of failures on our part. But God never stopped taking pleasure in us. In spite of ourselves, and though it caused him great grief, God remained attached to us.

I imagine that the people in exile found it hard to believe that God was delighting in them. The meditative story in chapter 3 suggested how the narrator laughed to think of cracked fingernails and the disarray of prison prompting someone to say "You are My Delight." The people felt rejected and undesirable. Their lands were ruined, their homes destroyed, the sacred temple sacked and burned, and the future of their children appeared to be one of slavery. They knew they had not worshiped with pure hearts nor lived in justice and compassion. A sense of unworthiness pervaded their thoughts. The little nation of people who had claimed that their God was lord of all had become the laughing stock of the known world.

But God had not abandoned them. There came through Isaiah the promise of a new identity. We have already considered that God sought them while they were far away and made a way to bring them home. Now we see the further results of that redeeming work:

> . . . you shall be called by a new name
> that the mouth of the LORD will give.
> You shall be a crown of beauty in the hand of the LORD,
> and a royal diadem in the hand of your God.
> You shall no more be termed Forsaken,
> and your land shall no more be termed Desolate;
> but you shall be called My Delight Is in Her,
> and your land Married;
> for the LORD delights in you,
> and your land shall be married.
>
> — Isaiah 62:2-4

The work of the promised Redeemer was to change the name of the Forsaken to My Delight Is in Her. This change was to be an objective transformation. The Hebrew literally means "it shall be called to you."[2] The accurate description of who you are as given by an outside, impartial observer will be that you are cherished by your God. The New Revised Standard translation of verse 4 adds an interesting dimension. The promised new names arise from God's *present* love "for the LORD delights in you," now, while you are far away, seemingly forsaken and exiled. This immediate pleasure while you are unworthy leads to a future glory caused by the loving work of the Anointed Redeemer.

GOD'S DELIGHT

This is tremendous good news! God delights in you right now. The situation of your life does not change his delight. The presence of doubt or a pattern of disobedience does not change God's pleasure in you. Right now he takes delight in your existence. You are his beloved, and his betrothed. You

---

[2] J. Alec Motyer, *The Prophecy of Isaiah*, p. 506.

appear to God as beautiful as a bride appears to her groom on the wedding day.

How can this be? Is God blind? or deluded? No, this is nothing less than the work of the promised Redeemer. Remember from the last chapter that the Redeemer does for the people what they cannot do. He brings them home, not only from physical exile, but to their God. He makes them called The Holy People because of his holiness that is given to them as a gift.

We have already seen that God seeks and finds us in Christ, calling us to him by name as a shepherd calls the sheep. Now we may see that our searching, redeeming God delights in us. He has restored the image of God within us by making us a new creation in Christ.

There is a divine pleasure in the work of redemption. God desired heartily to be among us in Jesus Christ. We read in the epistles, "For in [Jesus] all the fullness of God was *pleased* to dwell" (Col. 1:19, italics mine). Jesus in his teaching revealed God's disposition toward us. Once when a crowd had gathered around him, Jesus sought to reassure his disciples concerning their worries about daily bread and provisions. He said, "Do not be afraid, little flock, for it is your Father's good pleasure to give you the kingdom" (Luke 12:32). God took delight in offering us the splendor of his kingdom and the joy of life lived under his reign.

And such gifts were not given blindly. God knew the lot with whom he was getting mixed up. He knew that we would ultimately put Jesus to death, finding him too threatening to the part of us that wanted to stay lost. But he turned even our rejection into a work of love. Paul wrote to the Romans:

. . . God's love has been poured into our hearts through the Holy Spirit that has been given to us.

God proves his love for us in that while we still were sinners Christ died for us. For if while we were enemies, we were reconciled to God through the death of his Son, much more surely, having been reconciled, we will be saved by his life.

— Romans 5:5, 8, 10

Knowing full well who we have been, who we are, and who we will be, God became one of us in Jesus Christ. Understanding that though our souls ache for God, we also flee God, and knowing well the cost, Christ lived and died to be the Redeemer not only of Judah and Israel but the world.

THE PRESENT AND FUTURE

Discovering that God delights in us right now causes a change. We realize that the future is bright. We will grow in our ability to please God and respond to his love. We are motivated to improve right now. When people are loved in new ways, they begin to look different. There appears a glow, an inner joy which transforms the outward appearance. And they act better. We become as we are considered by those who matter the most. God's delight in us makes us become more delightful.

This joyful dynamic is expressed in the letter of 1 John where we read:

See what love the Father has given us, that we should be called children of God; and that is what we are. . . . Beloved, we are God's children now; what we will be has not yet been revealed. What we do know is this: when he is revealed, we will be like him, for we will see him as he is. And all who

have this hope in him purify themselves, just as he
is pure.

— 1 John 3:1-3

The passage radiates delight. Right now we are called
children of God because we really are the beloved children
of the great, all-loving Father. And this is only the
beginning. One day we will see God directly and that sight
will transforms us further into the image of God we were
created to be. Such hope, 1 John contends, is enough to
motivate us to get to work on the changes now. Realizing the
great love God has for us, we strive to mirror that love in our
daily lives.

Of course we are not nearly where we hope to be. The
long, difficult road of this life stretches between us and our
future with God. But we may draw on that future now in
order to assist us in growing into our new names. We live
today in what theologians call "the already and the not yet."
Already Christ has died and risen, already our sins are
forgiven and our redemption is sure. But not yet are the new
heavens and earth fully in place. Not yet are we all God has
made us to be. We live in the interim, and strive to take by
faith the names of promise. We pull into the *present* the
promises of what the *future* will be, based on what Christ
has done in the *past*.

In this way we see how the name Married applies to us.
Isaiah promised Judah that after the return the land would
be married. Many children would be born and they would
tend the land. A fertile partnership between God, the
people, and their land would yield a bountiful harvest.
Marriage has been long been a metaphor for the relationship
between Christ and the church. He cherishes us as a loving
husband, sacrificing himself for our well-being. Ephesians

tells us "Christ loved the church and gave himself up for her, in order to make her holy by cleansing her with the washing of water by the word, so as to present the church to himself in splendor, without a spot or wrinkle . . ." (5:25-27). Being named Married means that Jesus Christ has bound himself to us forever in a loving relationship. And the result of this wedding will be a fruitful, abundant life. The state of life described by a new name portends a rich harvest in the future.

The story of Abraham illustrates how the new names of promise could influence present life, even before the promises were completely fulfilled. In those days, Abraham was known as Abram, and Sarah was called Sarai. God promised Abram and Sarai that they would have descendants as numerous as the stars who would be a blessing to the entire earth. Abram believed the promises, but years passed without any sign of their fulfillment. When Abram was ninety-nine years old, the Lord appeared to him to reiterate the promises. It included a name change: "No longer shall your name be Abram, but your name shall be Abraham; for I have made you the ancestor of a multitude of nations" (Gen. 17:5). Abram's name meant "exalted ancestor." His new name meant "ancestor of a multitude." And from that moment on, the text uses the new name of Abraham—though the fulfillment of the promise was still more than a year away. He took the name of the promise into his present experience, and lived under its power and hope, even before the fulfillment came to pass.

So, we too may take the names God has promised now, in the present, though God is not finished with us yet, and though we do not reflect their meaning in anything but a paltry form right now.

Feeling defeated, or ugly, or fat, or rejected, or repellent, we nevertheless claim, "My name is My Delight Is in Her." Though we have been anything but delightful in our behavior, we may realize that God sees us according to the salvation the Redeemer has accomplished for us and according to the transformation the Holy Spirit is working within us.

RECEIVING THE NEW NAMES

In the middle of Isaiah 62, we are given further instruction on how to make the promised names part of present experience. We can add it to the activities of Isaiah 56 which we discussed in chapter 2. Now, in addition to the faith which holds fast to the covenant, the people were to make intercession. They were called to prayers of watching and prayers of asking:

> Upon your walls, O Jerusalem,
> I have posted sentinels;
> all day and all night
> they shall never be silent.
> You who remind the LORD, take no rest,
> and give him no rest until he establishes Jerusalem
> and makes it renowned throughout the earth (62:6-7).

These watchers on the walls were to take no rest in their intercessions, and give the Lord no rest until what he promised came to pass. They were to continually remind God of the new names offered to the people of Jerusalem.

Prayer is essential to living under the new names of God. We watch in prayer as we receive the new names through our reading of the scriptures and our meditation on those passages. Then we remind God in prayer as we claim them as our own, going on to pray constantly for God to fulfill the promise in our names. You might find these prayers a helpful start.

Gracious God,

You name me Sought Out. So, keep seeking me. Do not let me wander too far from you. Come find me when I take the wings of the dawn and flee to the uttermost regions of the earth. Even there let me find your presence and your guidance. Tether me to you. Do not let me get lost. Cast me not away from your presence. Though I run, come after me. Though I squirm, seek me out.

Gracious God,

You name me as part of the Holy People, The Redeemed of the Lord. Redeem me even now. Make me experience the freedom from the powers of diminishment, sin, and death. Buy me back every moment from the voices that tell me I am nothing. Unchain me from the destructive patterns of behavior I am powerless to stop. Call me apart from the world I love so much so that I may live as part of your holy, separate people.

Gracious God,

You call me your Delight. Look upon me and see not the foolish, selfish things I have done. But see the one for whom you died, the one for whom you intercede. See the object of your affection and make me to know that you are pleased to offer me the kingdom, especially when I worry.

Gracious God,

You call the land of my life Married. Make it so. Make a fruitful marriage between my inner and outer lives that produces a rich harvest of spiritual fruit and goodness in the world. Make me to know that being Married, my life has purpose and makes a difference in the world. Let the land of my life be fruitful. Make it content because I know you have sacrificed for me, and I know that I am cherished, through Christ my Redeemer.

The essential identity of the Christian, of the follower of Christ, is that you are continually Sought Out. You are desired and wanted in the presence of God. You are Redeemed of the Lord. God has done for you what you could not do for yourself. He has procured forgiveness and sent his Spirit into your heart, enabling you now to want to do his will even when you do not want to. You are God's Delight. He takes pleasure in your existence and your transformation. You, right now, are pleasing to God through Christ. You are unique and beloved. You are Married to God. In partnership with him, the land of your life is bringing forth a rich, bountiful harvest. We can receive the names by wearing God out in prayer until, like Abraham, the promise is fulfilled in our present experience.

Of course, redeeming us, naming us precious and beloved, is not merely for ourselves. God saved us for a purpose. We are to glorify him, and we have a work in the world to do. The names of our work for God will be considered in the next section.

PART THREE

RECEIVING THE NAMES OF THE WORK GOD CALLS US TO DO

CHAPTER 7

THE VOICE
SPEAKS A WORK

After the Voice calls us home from exile, we discover that we have a work to do for God in the world. The following meditation is a prelude to the chapters on the names that convey to us these tasks of service we have been given. For an image of the ruins to be restored, I saw in my imagination the shells of the border abbeys in Scotland. When Henry VIII decreed the dissolution of the monasteries in 1536, his soldiers ransacked these ancient holy places throughout Britain. In many, only the walls were left, presumably because they were too strong to tear down easily.

Today, the ruins of these abbeys are quite beautiful. They still retain an atmosphere of solace, though the grass grows where once there was paved floor and blue sky appears through the broken arches. I invite you to begin your thoughts on the work of rebuilding which follows exile with this imaginary continuation of the story begun in chapter 1. You may wish to return to it again after you have considered the new names of the work God gives us to do.

REBUILDING THE RUINS

Suddenly your exile is over. You are free to go. The nightmare ends and a new dream begins.

Rising from sleep, you find that you are walking up a broad, grassy hill. The skies above are blue and the wind is balmy. There are larger hills and woods in the distance. There is a pack on your back, with food, water, cooking supplies and a bedroll. In spite of its weight, you walk with freedom of movement and strong, deep breath. It feels as if you have been walking this land all your life.

At the top of the hill is a stone sanctuary. Gothic arches run along the sides toward a larger arch in the front. As you approach, you notice that you can see into the sanctuary, and through the arches to the blue sky. The sanctuary has no window glass and no roof.

All that remains is the outline of a church. The walls run along either side, a crumbling tower stands over the chancel. Amidst the floor of what was once the nave, grass grows amidst the scattered stones. Birds chirp from nests in the nooks of the arches. You can look all the way through the nave, through the choir, out the front towards the plain of the hill and then the woods. This is the outline of the sanctuary of an abbey ruined long ago.

You wonder why you are here and to what purpose. Then, the Voice that sang to you long ago comes again. Once you had been a captive, and the Voice sang to you new names, "My Delight Is in You. You are Sought Out and your land is Married." For a long time you have lived in that hope. Now, somehow, you have been translated to a new place and the Voice addresses you.

"Hephzibah," it calls, "I have another name for you. You will be called the Repairer of the Breach, the Restorer of Streets to Live In. For you will build upon the ancient foundations and restore that which has fallen into ruin. Out of the sharp places you will make gardens of peace. The people who live huddled in broken corners will return to homes of pleasant dwelling. I name you Repairer."

You look around now at the scattered stones. You walk over to the walls and check the foundations. They are built upon rock that is still solid. But it will be a long time before the space can be enclosed as a sanctuary again. Nevertheless, the Voice sang in your soul, and you are willing to do the work.

As your eyes survey the project, you discover that tools have been left near the front, where the altar once stood. There is a wheelbarrow, and even gloves. So you set to work removing rubble. The work is tiring, but satisfies you deeply.

The sun begins to set on your first day in the ruins. You feel quite free to rest when day is done. There is no hurry when you are committed to the whole task. You give thanks for the food and water in your pack, and the bedroll welcomes your body into sleep.

The next morning you rise and give thanks for the day. You bless the Voice which sang you your task. After breakfast you begin your clearing amidst the sound of birds and a light breeze. Strength you never had before surges through your muscles. You work with wholehearted abandon and joy.

This is why it takes a minute to acknowledge the scuffling you hear amongst the ruined choir. It is the first unnatural sound you have heard. You hurry over to your pack, check it, and realize that food is missing. Now you can feel your heart beating in your chest, and the hair on your skin is prickling. There could be danger.

But you have to know who, or what, took your food. You are angry and curious and know that until this is resolved, there can be no further work. So you walk slowly into the area that was once the choir. It is shadowed under the ruined tower above it.

You hadn't realized how many places there are to hide. As you peer into a dark corner, you hear a stone scuttle behind you. You turn around quickly and just catch a glimpse of a man in rags rushing toward you. Before there is time to move, he has you by the collar. He puts his filthy face right up to yours. His breath reeks and his eyes are wild. His fingers grip like a vise.

"I'll have that pack of yours now, and then I'll have you if you don't leave. This place is mine, and there's no room for you. Get out or you'll be mine."

Part of you is ready to run. Your mind is working at full speed now. Of course you should go. You don't belong here. Who were you to think you could rebuild the ruins. Oh, you want to be home and away from this man with rage all over his face.

But another part of you is anchored to the spot. You remember the Voice which sang your name. For months it sang to you when there was no hope and it sustained you until your life was restored from exile. Now the Voice has sent you here to work. And you will not turn from the call, and you will not die at the hands of this man. You simply will not.

Adrenaline rushes through you. A courage not your own works in your muscles, speaks through your mouth. Your hands reach up and slip under the man's arms. You lift him from the ground and pull his face even closer to yours than it was. You suck in his foul breath. You lock his eyes to yours.

"No," you say. "You will not harm me. You will not take my pack. I will not leave. This place does not belong to you, nor to me. It belongs to the one who sings with the Voice in the night. That One has sent me here to repair the ruins. I will not leave. I will do the work."

The man's face blanches. All the fight goes out of him. He has not been dealt with this way before. You continue, "Now, I will share what is in my pack with you. I feel quite certain there will be more than enough for both of us if we do not get greedy. I would welcome your help in this work. I will keep my distance at night and you may sleep where you always have. We can do this together if you like, but I am going nowhere."

Without a word, the man turns and bids you follow. In a space under that tower that must once have been the vestry, there is a family huddled. Three children and their mother are all dressed in rags, filthy and fearful. They seem as broken as these ruins and as defiant as the stone foundations enduring the seasons until restoration should occur.

"I have food," you begin. The words seem to come as much from the Voice as from you. "And water. And if I'm not mistaken, those who take up the work of repairing this sanctuary will find in the pack all that they need to be sustained. Join me. I need help. The stones are too heavy to lift alone, and truthfully, I haven't the skill to build by myself."

By the end of the afternoon, the family has helped you to clear rubble from a large section in the front of the nave. You sit down together for a meal. Within your pack there is more food.

And there are bedrolls for all. Whatever is needed is supplied. That evening, in the late summer sun, the six of you find a stream with a cold, deep pool where the children can play and all can bathe. In the morning all rise with thanksgiving.

Day by day the work of rebuilding continues. Each week, people arrive from the surrounding countryside to take up their shovels and their trowels. Always there is enough water, enough food, sufficient clothing. Only when someone tries to take too much is there a problem. Occasionally you have to confront those who view your little band as easy pickings. The message comes from the Voice and it is always the same: "We will share with you and we bid you join the work of raising these ruins. No, you may not have more than you need. You may not have this place for your own ends. We will not bend or yield to that demand. But if you wish to join the task given to us, you are welcome."

The weeks pass, and the sanctuary nears completion. The people worship within its walls daily. There are so many people that some have turned to the task of building homes along the grassy hill. A lovely garden is planted. The people have become a community. This is the work and the life for which you have longed. And so you live as the Repairer of the Breach, the Restorer of Streets to Live In. Day by day, you become what the Voice has named you to be.

CHAPTER 8

THE REPAIRER
OF THE BREACH

◆─◆◆◆─◆

. . . they shall repair the ruined cities,
the devastations of many generations.
— Isaiah 61:4

In the last section, we focused on the new names which
addressed our essential identity as people beloved of God.
Our starting point was the exile, the situation in which life
for the people of God got as bad as it could. The new names
came as an offer of sheer grace amidst hopelessness. So we
heard God declare that no matter where we are, no matter
how strongly we feel our name has become Forsaken, we are
continually Sought Out. Though we often feel unlovely and
unwanted, God promises that through grace we are ever
named My Delight Is in Her.

Now we will consider names associated with the
response we make to having this new identity. We are called
by name not only for our own redemption but so that we may
now join with God in offering this grace to the world. In
Isaiah 58, we will see that the people have a work of
restoration to perform. And the promised new names are not
given as unconditionally as in Isaiah 62. Rather, they are
given when the spirituality of the people is expressed not
just in religious exercises but in works of compassion. The
prophet writes:

> Your ancient ruins shall be rebuilt; you shall raise
> up the foundations of many generations; you shall be
> called the repairer of the breach, the restorer of
> streets to live in (58:12).

The word *breach* is an old word that refers to a gap or break. It is used infrequently these days, but still stirring in its effect. A whale does not just leap from the water. It "breaches" the surface, because so great is the ocean-going mammal that the very sea is split with its rising. We speak of a "breach" in trust, and though we mean that the trust is broken, "breach" implies a greater violation.

In the days of walled cities and castles, a breach in the fortifications meant a crisis. An invading army tried to create or find any breach in the walls to make its advance. Hence the phrase "standing in the breach" meant placing a human body in the gap where there once was solid wall. The person stood in the way of an onslaught, protecting all that was behind as though becoming part of the wall itself.

From the beginning this phrase has had more than a literal meaning. In Psalm 106, we read that Moses "stood in the breach" for the Hebrews after they had worshiped the Golden Calf (Psalm 106:23). The Lord was ready to destroy the people and start again, but Moses stood in the way of that wrath. He stood in the breach, and persuaded God to turn aside his anger.

If you say, "I'll be standing in the breach for you," you mean that you will be trying to fill in the gaps, to meet the needs, cover the blind spots, protect and defend. It moves me to think of the tired, battered defender standing in the breach so that those behind the walls may be kept safe. In Shakespeare's *Henry the Fifth*, the king cries out at the battle of Halfleur, "Once more unto the breach, dear friends, once more,/Or close the wall up with our English dead." (*Henry the Fifth*, III, i, 1–2). It was the English army which was attacking, but so vastly outnumbered were they, and so driven by courage and divine inspiration, that the words have the same effect. Once more unto the breach, to the place of danger, to the gap where life is won or lost.

The people, then, were promised the name of those who fill in the gaps created by human need. Literally the people would return to Jerusalem to rebuild the ancient walls. Symbolically, they were called to much greater works of repair. Called home in the joy of the names of grace, they would find their continuing experience of God through living out their names of Repairer of the Breach.

THE PARADOX IN OUR WORK FOR GOD

Here we arrive at one of the mysteries of our faith. God's love is unconditional and freely given. He names us his beloved even when we are as far from him as we could possibly get. Christ's death was for the sins of the whole world. Such grace can never be earned, manipulated or lost. We simply receive in faith. As Paul wrote to the Ephesians, "For by grace you have been saved through faith, and this is not your own doing; it is the gift of God—not the results of works, so that no one may boast" (2:8-9). Even our ability to believe is a gift. All that we do, we do in the strength God has given us; self-sufficiency is impossible.

And yet, here is the paradox. Though we do not work to gain God's love nor can we work in our own strength, we are nevertheless called to works of service. And our spiritual health and experience of God's grace is directly affected by our level of faithfulness in this service. Paul went on to say, "For we are what he has made us, created in Christ Jesus for good works, which God prepared beforehand to be our way of life" (Eph. 2:10). God works in us so that we might do the work of God in the world.

Isaiah 58 records the people complaining that their spirituality was not working. They were doing the religious thing. They fasted and prayed and went to worship. But they did not feel like they were getting through to God. They believed it was God's problem. The Lord replied:

> Look, you serve your own interest on your fast day,
> and oppress all your workers.
> Look, you fast only to quarrel and to fight . . .
> Is not this the fast that I choose:
> to loose the bonds of injustice . . .
> and to break every yoke?
> Is it not to share your bread with the hungry,
> and bring the homeless poor into your house;
> when you see the naked, to cover them,
> and not to hide yourself from your own kin? (58:3-4, 6-7).

Our relationship with God is intimately linked to our expressions of love to others, particularly those in acute need. Spirituality without service is an empty shell. But worse, this is not just a moral dilemma. While God's love for us never changes, our experience of God's love dries up if we are not passing along that love to a broken world. There is quite a bit of selfish motivation in becoming selfless people.

The Lord goes on to give them some incentive to move beyond themselves:

> Your light shall break forth like the dawn,
> and your healing shall spring up quickly . . .
> If you offer your food to the hungry

and satisfy the needs of the afflicted . . .
The LORD will guide you continually,
and satisfy your needs in parched places (58:8, 10-11).

Our comfort and our healing, our spiritual satisfaction is connected to our willingness to be conduits for the love of God. Our souls require for their own health that we extend ourselves to others. So it is in the context of feeding the hungry and clothing the naked that the people will be able to rebuild the ancient ruins and receive their new names. These names will arise as a result of faithful service.

LIVING OUT THE NAMES

Of course, names not only express what someone has been, but help to create what someone will do. Imagining ourselves now as bearing the name "Repairer of the Breach" on the basis of God's promise can help us to act in keeping with that identity. We pull the prophecy from the future into the present. We try on the name and look at the world through the eyes of someone described by it.

Our plans would be shaped by the question, "Where are the gaps I am called to fill today?" We enter the world in search of the ruins we are called to rebuild.

The vocation associated with our names from God becomes more important than what we do to make a living or pass the time. These names shape our view of the world. We consider daily how we who are God's Delight can express such a love to a world whose streets are torn. This work is to flow within every contact we have with another person. It is to run underneath everything that we do. We imagine ourselves not according to the many titles people give to us but as those named "Restorer of Streets to Live In." And so all we do is transformed.

For instance, you may return home one afternoon and walk into a maelstrom of accusations. "He broke my Legos!" "She hit me first!" "I hate him; he never leaves me alone." Your first instinct may be to sit on both of them, to solve the situation by overpowering it. But then you remember, "My name is Repairer. There are broken walls here. There is a gap in this relationship. How I can fill it?" And so you breathe deeply and begin to sort it out with patience and fairness.

One night the last thing in the world you want to do may be talking to someone who needs you. You're tired. You don't want to share. You don't want to listen. Surely one more day of silence could go by with no further damage done. This relationship has lasted so far; it will keep tonight. But you remember, "My name is Restorer of Streets to Live In. Livable streets contain pleasant places of interchange. People look after each other on such streets. So tonight, not tomorrow, I will listen and share."

Off to visit for your church the boring homebound person whom you have put off time and again, you can transform the encounter from life sapping drudgery to enervating encounter. On the way, you begin to think, "What is the breach in her life? There is a hole ripped within from the loss of her husband. I will try to stand in the breach for her for these moments. I will try to close the gap between her life and the encroaching loneliness that threatens her with despair. For my name is Repairer of the Breach."

Frustrated with the lack of response of the students to the mentoring program at your church, and facing a group of volunteers who are equally frustrated, tired, and on the edge of quitting, you can breathe these names into your task. You suggest that the group consider the broken streets of these children, and how unlivable have been their dwellings. Then you recall together that you are the Restorer of Streets to Live In. And you know from working on houses that most of the hard work is preparing the surface. Hours are spent removing nails, sanding rough places, replacing rotted wood. It is only after all the painstaking work that the second coat of paint finally goes on and makes the home look restored. So you help your fellow tutors set their sights on simply being a smooth, sanded presence in the midst of a rough life. You aim simply to remove one nail at a time, one section of cracked paint, one pile of rubble from your students' lives.

STRETCHING

In these and many other ways, we can grow in realizing how we are called to notice breaches in our daily lives, in our community, and in our world. We are called to see them and to fill the gaps. The level of our restoring work will vary among us. The more we have received the names of our identity as those whom God redeems, the more we will be able to bring that grace to others. Each of us, though, could grow into our new names a bit more by stretching ourselves in such service. By using the example of caring for needy children, we can explore the various levels of opportunity available to us.

For a person who has always been tightfisted with money, it may be a significant step to "adopt" a child by committing to monthly donations to a relief agency. Such an act will be a spiritual move expressed in financial terms. And it will help to close the breach in a child's care.

For others of us, however, such giving would not be a stretch at all. Something more tangible may be required.

One person with limited mobility may simply be able to knit caps which are sent overseas on the Hope ship. Another may be called to spend an hour a week mentoring a neglected youth. Others might be called to open their homes for emergency foster care. And some may fulfill their name as Repairers and Restorers by adopting a handicapped child.

The specific level of work depends on the nudgings of God's Spirit. We are all sent to different streets for the work of renovation. A good gauge of whether you are doing the right level of work to fulfill your name may be to consider if your service is resulting in the promised healing and intimacy with God. For as Isaiah promised, many people have found joy through the labor of standing in the breach for others.

A DANGER IN THE LABOR

There is a warning, however, in this call to extend ourselves. More than a few of us long to be the rescuers and the saviors. We'd gladly give our lives to stand in the breach. Just call, and I'll be at the hospital all night with you. Tell me your problems and I'll carry them for you, no matter how heavy the weight. Let's make shelters for the homeless and ladle soup for the hungry. We're ready to do anything.

The promise is that if we open our hands and our hearts to the needy, then our healing will rise like the sun, and our souls will be satisfied even in a sunscorched land. But some of us super workers have opened ourselves as fully as possible, and we are still empty. We are exhausted. Many of us are on the edge of burnout. We've been to the breach year after year. And still the onslaught keeps coming. No one comes to take a shift on our behalf. We're tottering, and we're angry, and one more blow could send us tumbling down.

So how do we fulfill the names given to us by this text—Repairer and Restorer—without nurturing a messiah complex and spending up our health and strength?

Fortunately, Isaiah 58 does not end with the task of ministry but with the task of rest. The prophecy continues:

> If you refrain from trampling the sabbath,
> from pursuing your own interests on my holy day;
> if you call the sabbath a delight . . .
> if you honor it, not going your own ways,
> serving your own interests, or pursuing your own affairs;
> then you shall take delight in the LORD,
> and I will make you ride upon the heights of the
>   earth (58:13-14).

The sabbath was instituted so that we might remember who is God. It was given to provide a decisive, mandatory break in the flow of work so that we might recognize that we are not indispensable. God's people rest, and the world keeps turning, because God, not we, is in control.

We do not need to wrangle here over which day certain professions should take for a sabbath or how necessary it is that hospitals and power plants operate continuously. The point is that purposeful rest to acknowledge God and refresh ourselves is just as important as the work of repair and restoration in the world.

In this time apart, we receive the identity that God gives us by grace. As we saw in chapter 2, the aliens and disfigured received their new names in part because of their observation of the Lord's sabbath. So we too have time on the sabbath to listen to the Spirit which names us Delight and Sought After. We understand that we do not serve in order to gain favor; we serve in response to the love we have already received. Then we are refreshed to take up the tasks God gives his people.

Spirituality without service is empty. By the same token, service without the spiritual discipline of rest leads to the idolatry of a savior complex on the one hand or burnout on the other. The Repairers of the Breach are called to take a day to worship the master builder, the true savior. There is no substitute for ceasing our labors a whole day a week. There is no substitute for taking the time to acknowledge the one God. These forms of spiritual restoration make the restoring work on the front lines of the breach possible.

When we see our work through the names God gives us, we can find fresh motivation for the task. When we discipline ourselves for the kind of rest which returns control of the work to the Creator, then we remain in touch with our identity as God's beloved. Instead of burning out, we replenish, and our souls stand ready to respond to the clarion call of the High King of Heaven which sounds, "Once more unto the breach, dear friends, once more."

CHAPTER 9

OAKS OF
RIGHTEOUSNESS

———— ◆·◆·◆ ————

Then shall all the trees of the forest sing
for joy.

— Psalm 96:12

If you've ever worked on renovating a house, you know that "repairing the ruins" is an arduous task, full of dirt, bruises, sweat, and exhaustion. The names of our work for God include such active labor, as we saw in the last chapter. The next pair of names, however, describes a service that appears to be much more passive though no less significant in effect. These names arise more from the effort required in sabbath rest than the from the work of construction. Isaiah 61 declares, "They will be called oaks of righteousness, the planting of the LORD, to the display of his glory" (61:3).

The people of God are promised that the world will describe them in terms of trees in an orchard. Trees are lovely to look at, but at first thought, they do not seem mobile enough to be an apt metaphor for all the work the people of God need to do in the world. An orchard does not move from where it is planted. A garden does not go to work rebuilding ruined cities. But if we think more deeply, we can understand the vital activity of trees in the restoration of the world.

A stationary tree, almost motionless on a calm day, is alive with activity. Its roots sink deep into the soil to search for moisture and anchor the tree against the winds of the world. In the process, these roots may burrow through rock and reshape the earth where the tree is planted. And they brace the ground with their grip against erosion, preserving the landscape.

Its branches reach for sunlight so their leaves may enact the miracle of photosynthesis. In the process, carbon dioxide becomes oxygen, the air is renewed, and all animal life benefits. Trees do not usually grow in isolation but tend naturally towards the community of the forest, which has its own cycles of life. During the summer, the canopy of leaves in a forest provides relief from the heat. These leaves fall to the ground in the autumn. Those not taken by squirrels for nests decay to nourish the soil in which the tree lives.

Nuts and fruit from certain trees feed people and woodland animals. Blossoms in the spring attract insects which spread seeds to other areas. These fatten insects become food for the birds who nest in the tree's branches. Trees teem with activity, and participate in sustaining the life cycles of the world. But they do so in place, without "toiling or spinning" as Jesus said. Healthy trees simply enact what they are in relationship to the environment in which they were planted.

GROWN IN GOD'S GARDEN

Isaiah envisioned the redeemed people as the result of God's own gardening efforts in the world: "They are the shoot that I planted, the work of my hands, so that I might be glorified" (60:21). The Lord is the soil in which we grow. He nourishes us with his life so that we become what we were made to be.

God is the garden and his soil is filled with righteousness. This means that if our lives are grown in God, there will be an essential rightness, a wholeness, in all our living. We will be moving towards an organic relationship with God.

Like trees we will take in the life and light he gives us and give out (metaphorically) oxygen, fruit, and shade which pleases God and sustains the world. God will grow up through us, causing us to be at peace with ourselves and transforming our relationship with others. The flourishing trees in the Lord's garden thus become a display of God's glory for the world to see. At the end of chapter 61, we read:

> For as the earth brings forth its shoots,
> and as a garden causes what is sown in it to spring up,
> so the Lord God will cause righteousness and praise
> to spring up before all the nations (61:11).

God works in us to cause us to spring up with righteousness and praise. Growing in God's garden, we glorify him. Being what God makes us, we show forth his praise.

As we saw beginning in chapter 5, this transformation in us is the work of the promised Redeemer. Through Jesus, God grows in us the new names which we cannot produce on our own.

ABIDING IN THE VINE

But we have a part to play that is crucial to the growing of the orchard of God. We cooperate. We invite and allow and encourage God to do his work of redemption in us. This seems like a very passive activity. We do not try to achieve our righteousness. We receive the righteousness of Jesus, the Anointed One, so that it can grow through us as the nourishment from good soil flows up through the roots throughout a tree.

Jesus elaborated on this image of being a planting of the Lord in John 15. His illustration revolved around the concept of abiding. To abide means to dwell or remain in a certain place or condition. It is a word for a kind of active passivity in which we allow God to be in us what he desires.[3] We simply consent to remain as God has made us, to be conduits for what God does within us. Jesus said:

> Abide in me as I abide in you. Just as the branch cannot bear fruit by itself unless it abides in the vine, neither can you unless you abide in me. I am the vine, you are the branches. Those who abide in me and I in them bear much fruit, because apart from me you can do nothing. My Father is glorified by this, that you bear much fruit and become my disciples.
> — John 15:4-5, 8

The illustration is of a relationship. There is interchange between the vine and its branches. A kind of mutual indwelling occurs. Jesus is in us and we are in Jesus. Christ flows through us and we produce fruit which glorifies God. Our part is cooperation, a consent of the will that invites and allows God to shape us as he wills.

So in Isaiah 61, the righteousness brought by the Anointed One is grown in the people of God and they are named Oaks of Righteousness, the Planting of the Lord. Scholars note that "oaks" is not limited to one kind of tree but actually refers to any kind of large tree.[4] So, some

---

[3]For further reference on abiding in the vine read Andrew Murray's *Abide in Christ*.

[4]Among others, J. Alec Motyer, *The Prophecy of Isaiah*, p. 501.

further references in scripture comparing us to trees and the fruit they produce may help us more fully receive these names.

DELIGHT IN THE LAW OF THE LORD

The first psalm begins by contrasting the scoffers of the world with the delighters. Those who live paying no deference to God, develop a mocking cynicism as they see, and participate in, the futile struggles of humanity. But those who sink their roots into the story of God's loving activity in the world, live with a blessed joy:

> Happy are those who do not follow the advice of
>   the wicked,
> or take the path that sinners tread,
> or sit in the seat of scoffers;
> but their delight is in the law of the LORD,
> and on his law they meditate day and night.
> They are like trees planted by streams of water,
> which yield their fruit in its season,
> and their leaves do not wither.
> In all that they do, they prosper.
>   — Psalm 1:1-3

If the soil of one's life is the way of the world as it is without God, then the harvest is one of hollow laughter, temporarily holding despair at bay. But if one is planted in the garden of God's love, the yield is a prospering fruitfulness in every endeavor.

Meditating on the law of God may be compared to sinking one's roots into soil that is next to a flowing stream. A continual source of nourishment waters the life. God's word gives us depth and texture. Without it, our perceptions are shallow. We only see the surface of reality. Plants in a pot have a limited range of growth. But trees in fertile soil may grow to their full potential. So when we reflect on life as having a deeper meaning than the usual hectic getting and spending, we tap into a source for flourishing. People who understand themselves as part of the great story of redemption God is telling in the world, live with a rootedness and a fruitfulness which blesses those around them.

Such spiritual depth may not seem at first like much of a service to a world in ruins. Then, as we meditate on the metaphor of trees, we may realize how we long to be near people of great faith and tenacious stability. I have seen great hemlocks growing next to rushing streams. Their roots wrap around the granite of the sides of the creek bed. They protect the entire hillside from eroding into the water so that younger trees may flourish above them. Their silent contribution to the forest endures for decades.

These "trees" are the people who hold churches together with their quiet faithfulness. Their presence maintains the praise of God in worship week after week, year after year. They enable whole communities to flourish by their integrity, their hard, productive work for decades, and their just dealings with all whom they meet. We may see in them marriages that last more than half a century. Without thinking about it, we count on the stability of their love as an anchor amidst the changes of life. They know how to love because they are deeply connected to the source of love.

They are the intercessors of the world. When they wake in the night, they do not curse the darkness but pray until they fall asleep again. How much of God's redemptive work has been accomplished through such prayers that no others ever know about? Without fanfare they read the scriptures day after day and are formed into trees in the garden of God. When we take time to listen to their wisdom, we can hear an understanding of the Bible that exceeds the greatest scholars.

They love young people and provide a sense of home for years to children of many families. Their houses are places of peace. A quiet atmosphere of order pervades. These are the ones who willingly do menial jobs of service in the church, home or community without complaint because they understand life in a larger context. They retain perspective through the years that others in their hurry often lose. Though not flamboyant, these are people of a vision that arises from meditating upon the law of the Lord.

Such work for God does not move about in search of broken streets to repair, but remains rooted in one place while the streets of healing are laid around them. This is the work of anchoring which arises from the name Oaks of Righteousness.

TRUST IN THE LORD

The great trees in a forest endure the first blasts of weather and spare the younger ones some of that stress. When blazing sun beats down in August, the tallest trees with the deepest roots survive the first waves of heat, shading those below them. The prophet Jeremiah, whose ministry followed Isaiah's, added an important aspect to this metaphor of trees planted by streams. He understood how important such people are in the midst of crisis. Jeremiah wrote:

> Blessed are those who trust in the LORD,
> whose trust is in the LORD.

They shall be like a tree planted by water,
sending out its roots by the stream.
It shall not fear when heat comes,
and its leaves shall stay green;
in the year of drought it is not anxious,
and it does not cease to bear fruit.
— Jeremiah 17:7-8

Those who are growing into their names as God's own planting provide a stabilizing effect to communities when afflictions come. These Oaks of trust in God exude a deep peace that calms those around them. When everything seems to fall apart, they stand firm and solid. Others lean upon them for strength and solace.

Such peacefulness cannot be fabricated. It is as organic as a living plant. For this calm arises from a long history of trust in God's faithfulness to provide in time of need. So when the years of drought come, these people of God do not scamper about in a panic. They do not need to rearrange their entire lives because they have already built them on a pattern of faithfulness which endures in good times and bad. They rejoice even in the midst of trial.

Their presence in our midst can hardly be overestimated. They perform a quiet work of healing in the world. We may find them laboring as physicians or gardeners, as therapists or secretaries. But we discern them when we are in trouble and need someone to whom we may turn for solace. With steady presence and quiet love, those who are named as God's Oaks maintain their rootedness in trusting God and so shade the others whose lives are blown about.

THE FRUIT OF THE SPIRIT

Finally, we turn to Paul's letter to the Galatian churches. He deepened the understanding of how cooperation with God's redemptive work leads to a rich harvest of blessing for the world. He knew that a large part of us desires only to do what we want to do, without reference to the will of God. Such cooperation with our worst selves leads predictably to relationships of injustice and disfunction. But, considering oneself as a planting in the Lord's garden and yielding to the growth God desires to accomplish in us leads to fruitfulness. He wrote:

> By contrast, the fruit of the Spirit is love, joy, peace, patience, kindness, generosity, faithfulness, gentleness, and self-control. There is no law against such things. And those who belong to Christ Jesus have crucified the flesh with its passions and desires. If we live by the Spirit, let us also be guided by the Spirit.
>
> —Galatians 5:22-25

The Anointed Redeemer's work was to recreate us for his glory. We are freed to live now according to all we were meant to be. God's righteousness is within us through the Holy Spirit. It yearns for expression in the world. Paul urges us towards a harmony between the inner spirit and the outer works. We achieve such authenticity by yielding our wills to God. We cooperate with what God is doing in us. We consent to live as those renamed by God. And then bountiful fruit is created through us.

This at first seems so passive. We want to do something more active. But this deep spiritual cooperation is essential to being those whose lives glorify God in the world. We have seen that the names Oaks of righteousness and a Planting of the Lord grow in us when we meditate on God's story of love found in the scriptures and rely wholeheartedly on the love of God amidst the various circumstances of life. Becoming those who are rooted and grounded in such grace provides a greater service to the world than we may ever realize.

CHAPTER 10

PRIESTS OF
THE LORD

*. . . like living stones, let yourselves be
built into a spiritual house, to be a
holy priesthood . . .*

— 1 Peter 2:5

There is a difference between people who have learned their
names from God and those who have not. Those who have
taken to themselves the joy of being God's Delight because
they are the Redeemed of the Lord have a growing sense of
confidence and purpose. These Oaks of God also have an
increasing awareness of their responsibility to be Restorers
of Streets as they share in God's work of greening and
repairing again the parched and broken world. We recoil,
though, from any sense of superiority that people of faith
might have over others. We do not want to act as if we are
better. We know we are not. But there remains a difference.
The people who know they are named by God have
something for which the rest of the world yearns. The story
of God's redeeming, renaming love is ours to share.
Acknowledging that distinction is not triumphalism. It is a
call to ministry.

The next pair of names in Isaiah 61 address this role
that the named of God have in the world: "but you shall be
called priests of the LORD, you shall be named ministers of

our God" (61:6). The people of Judah were promised that they would be recalled from the discard pile of exile to a place of central importance to the world. They would at last fulfill a role foretold to Abraham and Sarah: "by your offspring shall all the nations of the earth gain blessing for themselves, because you have obeyed my voice" (Gen. 22:18). This role was restated after the Exodus: "Indeed, the whole earth is mine, but you shall be for me a priestly kingdom and a holy nation" (Exod. 19:5-6).

God's interest is in the redemption of all people. But he has offered this grace by first calling apart a particular people from the rest of the world. God has used those who have taken their new names to communicate his love to those who have yet to discover all that God names them. We do not know why some respond sooner than others, or why God chooses one person and not another for this task. This will remain a mystery through all our days on earth. But it is still a fact. Some people "get it" before others. They receive the joy of knowing God and the burden of being in his service. There is both privilege and responsibility. As we consider what it means to be named Ministers of our God, we are careful never to separate this duty and the honor.

THE ROLE OF PRIESTS

In ancient Judah, the priests functioned as intermediaries between God and the people. They offered animal sacrifices on the altar to atone for the sins of the people and restore them to fellowship with God. On behalf of the ordinary people, the priests went to God and returned to them with news of God's forgiveness. They also offered daily sacrifices as signs of thanksgiving and devotion.

The priests were those who maintained the house of

God and the worship which took place there. It was their responsibility to read, memorize, meditate upon, and interpret the word of God. They pronounced cleansing of those who had been defiled, often judged in disputes between people, and oversaw the important passages of life: offerings of thanks at birth, circumcisions for males, marriages, burials.

As compensation for this life of service, the priests were afforded special privileges. They did not own land as the other tribes of Israel, but received offerings from the people. The tribe of Levi was the priestly tribe and so the priesthood of Israel was called the "Levitical" priesthood. Of course, any privilege can lead to abuse. All human institutions manifest our tendency toward greed and selfish control. But the Levites were set apart to perform a crucial role among the people of God. They maintained the people's sense that the central reality of their lives was the story of God working through them. The priests upheld their identity as a nation God had particularly called and blessed, and sent into the world to be witnesses to the one God.

JESUS IS OUR HIGH PRIEST

As the first Christians understood the Anointed Redeemer of Isaiah to be Jesus, they also recognized that Jesus is the ultimate priest for the world. He offered himself on the world's behalf, in spending his energies on teaching, healing, praying, and by giving up his life on the cross. We have always recalled Jesus' words from the Last Supper as the offering of himself on behalf of the world: "This is my body that is for you. . . . This cup is the new covenant in my blood" (1 Cor. 11:24-25). Jesus performed a priestly function in bridging the gap between God and humanity.

Through him, we have "access to God in boldness and confidence" (Eph. 3:12).

The book of Hebrews elaborates on this understanding of Jesus as our continuing priest. It makes many connections between the work of Christ and the functions of the Levitical priesthood. The seventh chapter summarizes the thinking, and for clarity I have rearranged one verse:

> For it is fitting that we should have such a high priest, holy, blameless, undefiled, separated from sinners, and exalted above the heavens. Unlike the other high priests, he has no need to offer sacrifices day after day, first for his own sins, and then for those of the people; this he did once for all when he offered himself. . . . Consequently, he is able for all time to save those who approach God through him, since he always lives to make intercession for them.
>
> — Hebrews 7:26-27, 25

The priesthood of Jesus was enacted once for all in the giving of himself on the cross. That death, mysteriously, made a way of peace for all time between humanity and God. But Jesus' priestly work continues even now in that he continues to pray for us.

Here we are before the mystery of the Triune God. Jesus remains fully God and fully human. As God, he offers himself to be known and worshiped in love. As a human being, he leads our worship, offering his obedience and faithfulness on our behalf. The salvation he achieved for us, he continues to work out in us. Through Christ, our sins are forgiven and our relationship with God is restored. From that base, God continues to grow us towards being all we were originally created to be. We are being steadily, surely conformed to the image of Christ. I find great joy in realizing that Jesus is working as a priest on my behalf even now. He intercedes for us. He prays for our continued experience of God's great love and salvation.[5]

THE PRIESTHOOD OF ALL BELIEVERS

Christians historically have also understood that the work of the Levitical priesthood has been broadened to be a task for all believers. Following in the stream of Isaiah, we realize that we are called to go to God on behalf of the world. And we go to the world on God's behalf. The letter of 1 Peter understood the community of believers to be a spiritual temple for the worship of God. Within that community we all function as priests through our prayers, worship, and proclamation of the story of Christ. We read:

> . . . let yourselves be built into a spiritual house, to be a holy priesthood, to offer spiritual sacrifices acceptable to God through Jesus Christ. You are a chosen race, a royal priesthood, a holy nation, God's own people, in order that you may proclaim the mighty acts of him who called you out of darkness into his marvelous light.
>
> — 1 Peter 2:5, 9

The reason we are given such a privileged title is so that we may proclaim God's mighty acts of mercy toward us to the world. We have been named by God in order that we might pass along those names to others. We can consider

---

[5]For more on the subject of Jesus' priesthood, see James Torrance, *Worship, Community and the Triune God of Grace*, Downers Grove: InterVarsity Christian Press.

how this ministerial work is accomplished by looking more closely at three functions of priesthood we all perform: worship, intercession, and proclamation.

WORSHIP

In my Presbyterian tradition, one of the great ends of the church is described as "the maintenance of divine worship." We are called to keep the praises of God continually flowing. The church all across the earth draws apart from the pace of the world to worship God. Of course this happens throughout the Lord's Day when, beginning at one point on the international dateline and sweeping west, the church brings forth a cascade of adoration. But it also happens throughout the world throughout the week whenever God's people gather as two or more to acknowledge Christ's lordship. At any given moment, somewhere on the planet, the God who has come to us in Jesus Christ is being exalted in worship.

We believe as well that our worship is merely a participation in the universal praise of God that is going on throughout creation. All things, simply in their existence, give glory to the creator. And those endowed with consciousness can add intentional praise. The church has maintained from the beginning that our voices merely join the heavenly chorus of spiritual beings who are forever singing God's praise. So when we worship at a given time, we are stepping into the stream of adoration that is ever flowing through the cosmos.

This drawing apart to worship is itself a service to the world. We hold forth to the world a different model of reality. The worshiping church declares that life is not, at the deepest level, simply about our immediate wants and needs.

Rather, we exist to glorify and serve the God who has made us. Though it may seem that everyone is going down a path of self-centered destruction, the church in its worship stands against that tide. We acknowledge the one true God who has made himself known in Jesus Christ. In that way, the church is a beacon to the world, drawing people to come out of the darkness to behold the light of Christ.

By our presence and participation in worship we bear witness to the world of our acknowledgement of God's reality. Though our focus is on God, we actually minister to the world because we declare hope amidst despair, the primacy of love over the forces of evil, and the gift of everlasting life in the face of so much death.

Vigorous worship takes work. Though we no longer have to offer animal sacrifices, we do make the sacrifice of time, energy, and attention. Our worshiping work as the Priests of God is encapsulated by the verse from Hebrews, "Through him, then, let us continually offer a sacrifice of praise to God, that is, the fruit of lips that confess his name" (Heb. 13:15). Confessing the name of Christ in public worship leads to fruit in the watching world.

INTERCESSION

Since we are named Priests of the Lord, we are to go continually before God on behalf of a world in ruins. As we saw in Isaiah 62, we are called to "remind the LORD, take no rest, and give him no rest until he establishes Jerusalem" (verses 6-7). Our work as priests is constantly to hold up to God the vision of the world he has promised. The biblical scholar J. Alec Motyer has commented on this persistence: "We do not conclude that otherwise [God] would forget, but that our prayers are, by his will, in some way a vital ingredient in the implementing of his promises."[6]

Looking upon the present wreckage of the world, we envision the world in which God's redemption has come to fruition. And we pray that it will come to be. Rather than be undone by a world that seems so far from Isaiah's hope, we cry out to God for his promised salvation to be accomplished against all odds. We priests are those who stand defiantly, almost insanely, against the present appearance of life in the world. We remember that things are supposed to be different, and we remind God that we have such a memory because of his own word. So in prayer we echo our Lord who taught us to pray imperatively, "Thy kingdom come, Thy will be done, on earth as it is in heaven."

This kind of intercession attempts to pull into the present the future that has been promised by God. We dare to pray so boldly because of what has already been accomplished by the Anointed Redeemer in the past. Such prayers span from supplications for the needs of one individual by a solitary prayer to petitions for all of humanity offered by the church universal. Every shred of intercession is part of our work as God's priests. We may pray about everything.

Christians in the Eastern Orthodox tradition have a very high understanding of the church's priestly work on behalf of the world in its worship. Catherine Aslanoff has written:

> The Church is the center of the universe; within it is accomplished the salvation of the world. . . . we offer to God, by means of the Holy Gifts, the visible and

---

[6]J. Alec Motyer, *The Prophecy of Isaiah*, 507.

invisible worlds, all creation, in these words:

> Your own of your own,
> we offer unto you
> on behalf of all
> and for all.

In the bread and wine which are offered and sanctified, Christ assembles the whole world, the cosmos, created by God with love and saved in his person.[7]

This stretches the limits of my understanding of what happens in worship. But through such a quotation, we can at least glimpse the magnitude of the task of intercession for the world which has been given to God's people. We offer the whole world up to God in prayer.

THE MINISTRY OF RECONCILIATION

In the first two priestly acts, we engage God through worship and intercession, and the world is affected by our spiritual service. In this third area, however, we who are the Ministers of our God engage the world more directly. We tell the story of our new names to those who have lived under the names of diminishment. As God has gracefully changed our names, we offer on his behalf the opportunity for others to receive the same new names. We do this as we tell how God came to the world in Jesus Christ and unfold the tale of all that was accomplished through his life, death, and resurrection.

---

[7]Catherine Aslanoff, *The Incarnate God*, volume II (Crestwood, NY: St. Vladimir's Seminary Press, 1995), 100, 101.

Paul explained this ministry clearly in his second letter to the Corinthian church. We can still feel the joy and excitement he has in passing along this good news. He wrote:

> . . . see, everything has become new! All this is from God, who reconciled us to himself through Christ, and has given us the ministry of reconciliation; that is, in Christ God was reconciling the world to himself, not counting their trespasses against them, and entrusting the message of reconciliation to us. So we are ambassadors for Christ, since God is making his appeal through us; we entreat you on behalf of Christ, be reconciled to God.
>
> — 2 Corinthians 5:17-20

We are named as God's own. We have received his marvelous love toward us in Jesus Christ. This news, however, was not meant to stop with us. We are sent to bring the story of this great love to the world.

Our message is to those who have labored so long under the names of defeat. We go to the foreigners and aliens, all the people who have felt excluded and unworthy for so long. We invite them to come in to the full welcome of our loving God. We take the word to the eunuchs, to all who have experienced life as dried up and without hope for the future. To these who have thought that God has forgotten them, we offer flowing, everlasting life in Jesus Christ. We invite them into the heart of our worship and prayer.

For reasons that remain a mystery, when there surely must be more reliable messengers, God nevertheless makes his appeal to the world through the likes of us. We are named as the Repairers of the Breach, and so we appeal to the world by concrete actions of restoration. God calls us the Lord's Own Planting, and so we appeal to the world by our quiet cooperation with what God is growing in us. And he calls us his Ministers and Priests. So we appeal to others by our prayers, our worship, and proclamation. We live into our new names when, in all these ways, we implore the world: Be reconciled to God!

PART FOUR

———•◦•———

RECEIVING THE NAMES
OF
OUR COMMUNITY

CHAPTER 11

THE VOICE
SHAPES A CITY

Once again, we return to the meditative story of the Voice that called an individual out of exile into the building of a community that worships God.

The work of repair continued. Soon there were so many people drawn to rebuilding these ruins that not all were needed for the sanctuary or the homes. These began to construct the walls that would surround what was quickly becoming a city.

There was no shortage of materials. For those who came to the City brought with them great gifts. Ships landed in the harbor with cargoes filled with strong, straight logs of pine and cypress. Their wood cutters quickly shaped these into beams for construction. Great loads of iron were hauled up the hill, and chests of silver and gold and bronze.

Soon lovely gates of bronze were raised. They were as strong as a mountain but looked as light as feathers, so fine was their construction. These gates stayed open day and night to welcome the pilgrims who arrived steadily every hour.

From the ramparts of the walls, you could look out to the sea. It thrilled your heart to see the great ships winging their way towards the harbor. Whole families came from great distances. And here in the city loved ones were united in joyful reunions. People who looked familiar to you were returning from exile. And strangers, odd people not at all like anyone you ever expected to meet also came.

There always seemed to be enough room. There certainly was enough food. For the pilgrims had come to stay. They brought with them herds of cattle and flocks of sheep. These grazed happily on the green hillsides. Rich stores of grain came, and seed for the planting that now took place outside the walls.

Of all the bustling life within the City, nothing was so glorious as the singing. You could hear it walking the lanes at any hour. Someone was always singing. They lifted their voices in praise to the Voice, the One who had spoken the vision of the City into being.

The people sang as they worked. The carpenter sang thanks to see a beam of wood cut and placed exactly into place. A farmer sang praise for the milk of the cows. Parents instructed children to follow the lead of the birds and chirp praise for the day upon rising. Those who drew water from wells sang of the fountain of all life. So many and varied and melodious were these voices that it seemed as if even the gates were echoing praise. The very walls of the City seemed to proclaim Deliverance. They sang to the people within of shelter and hope renewed, of peace and righteousness at last.

There were some to whom the Voice of the One came most often and most directly. These few readily admitted that their work was no more or less important than that of any other person. And yet all agreed that those who heard the Voice most clearly should direct the affairs of the City. Since the moment you heard the Voice sing to you in the night, through the tentative beginnings of restoration, you have known you are to be one of those devoted to hearing the Voice. Not only have you had to listen attentively, but you had to speak and sing for the Voice as accurately as possible. To you, with a few others, it had fallen to be the voice of the Voice for the people.

Whenever you spoke, the people hung on your words. Each syllable was precious news of the life in the City. To your own ears, though, your words always sounded inadequate. How could you ever speak the passion of the Voice that sang to you in the night? How could you ever get the words right? What translation was ever adequate?

It was a relief when others also began to hear and speak the words of the Voice. You joined as a council of Listeners. Together you tried to give words to what you heard that was beyond all words. Together you could correct and balance one another so that the translation was more accurate than it ever had been when you were alone.

Striving always to be faithful to the Voice, the council directed the affairs of the City. Most days this was a joy. The deepest crisis came, however, when some arrived who asked why there had to be any walls at all in this community of the blessed. They wanted to know why they had to pass through the gates, which were too narrow for all they had brought along. And they wanted to know why tribute was needed when the City seemed to have every-thing in abundance. Why couldn't they remain on the outside with their things while the City opened its walls before them?

The council strove together for many hours. Indeed, this was a City for the world. It seemed pointless to have any boundaries, especially when more people had to be accommodated every day. And it seemed ridiculous to demand such high tribute when there was no lack.

On the other side, several of the council noted that there had always been enough room within the walls, no matter how many new people came. The walls accommodated all who came within. And, they said, no matter the amount of tribute brought, no one had lacked for anything since the beginning, and no one ever had any more than was needed.

The deadlock was broken at last when one member proclaimed that the Voice had decreed the rebuilding of the ruins and the establishment of the walls. It was the Voice who motivated people to come bearing tribute. There had been no rules about amounts. It was understood, however, that to enter the City, people paid homage to the One whose Voice had sung it all into being.

And so the walls were kept. And the gates remained, though they were never closed. As you walked among the ramparts, you listened ever to the sound of the singing, and how beautiful it was echoing off the stones.

In fact, as the days went on, you noticed that as the singing magnified in the City, the light also was growing within.

The presence of the One was felt more keenly.

And the Voice began to be heard everywhere, singing love into every home, down every alley, within every one. The singing was heard and also seen as a growing, illuminating light.

Soon the lamps and torches were not lit at night. The City was lit with the presence of the One.

The council no longer met. The decision about the walls was their last one. For now everyone within the City heard the Voice clearly. All obeyed and all rejoiced.

Still the nations swept in on the seas and passed through the gates. Old, young, broken and whole, limping and leaping, of every hue and comportment they came.

This, you realized, was the beginning of the City of the Lord, which shall have no end.

CHAPTER 12

THE CITY
OF THE LORD

See, the home of God is among mortals.
He will dwell with them as their God;
they will be his peoples,
And God himself will be with them.
— Revelation 21:3

In this final section, we encounter a concept that has been implied from the beginning but not fully considered: The new names are given not just to individuals but to the people of God as a community. Of course, a true community arises only when its individuals intentionally enter committed relationships together. Each of us has significant work to do on the identity and tasks God gives us through the new names. But now, after undertaking to begin that personal work, we may unveil what has been true all along. We bear these names together and the goal is to become a City of the Lord.

God remains interested in each person individually. God considers us, though, not in isolation but in relationship to one another. We need one another in order to receive and fulfill our names from God. In fact, we name one another by the ways we interact. From the beginning, God has been laboring to redeem people as a family which bears his name. The boundaries of that family have been ever widening from the family of Noah to the small band that traveled with Abraham and Sarah to the tribes of Israel to the body of Christ, which is the church. This church universal is the community of people who bear God's name across the world and throughout all ages.

Isaiah saw beyond the remnants of the nations of Judah and Israel to a future vitality for God's people. We hear, ". . . they shall call you the City of the LORD, the Zion of the Holy One of Israel" (60:14). The promise in such a name is that God will fashion his people into a thriving, bustling community marked by relationships of love and peace. The presence of God in their midst will be so strong that the nations of the world will be drawn irresistibly to the City. There they will join the joyful worship of God that goes on continuously, satisfying human longing and transforming all relationships.

Cities today may have an identity based on sports teams, climate and scenery, industry, tourist attractions or even artistic opportunities. New York has theatre; Miami has beaches; Atlanta became an Olympic City in 1996. Isaiah envisioned the world adding to that list, "And Jerusalem has the Lord." He foresaw a city known throughout the world for the shining presence of God and the just, harmonious interactions of its citizens.

In the hope of this promise, we are not repairing the breach and restoring the streets simply so our property values will rise. Rather, we labor to build a model of the City of the Lord that is to come. The defining mark of our community is to be the felt presence of our loving, redeeming God. In our "city," any visitors should be able quickly to discern our Lord through our worship, our service, our conversation, and our love. So receiving this new name means working to bring Isaiah's future into the present.

THE VISION

Isaiah 60 records a wonderful vision of all the world streaming toward the holy City of the Lord. The scattered sons and daughters will return home. The rulers of the nations will come bearing gifts. And people from every land will seek the salvation contained within the walls of the City.

The inhabitants will look out from the walls and their hearts will "thrill and rejoice" (60:5) to see this home-coming. They will look out to the sea and observe the great ships flying along like clouds, like doves to their nests. In the cargo will be priceless tribute for the honor and glory of the Lord. On the decks will be those who shout praise when they at last glimpse the ramparts of the City and know they have found the joy of their desiring.

Within Holy Zion, the praise of God will never cease. The light of the sun and moon will no longer be needed because the brightness of the Lord's presence will shine upon the people. God will be their everlasting light. The days of sorrow will cease. Instead of ruin and destruction, peace will reign throughout. Righteousness—right dealing, equitable relating—will be the order of the day.

The God of the enslaved, exiled Hebrews will be revealed as the Lord of the universe. Salvation will be extended to all who desire to receive it. Zion's gates will stand open day and night to receive those who arrive: foreigners, eunuchs, exiles; the abused, the excluded, the neglected; rich, poor, and in between; the power brokers and the pawns; prisoners, hungry, sick, and lame; old and young. The joy of the Holy City is for all people. All the former categories of division fall away. This will be the reign of God.

THY KINGDOM COME

A Zionist, either Christian or Jewish, might take this vision literally, as if it referred to the future of the very city of Jerusalem we may visit today in Israel. I believe, however, that Isaiah is referring not only to the Jerusalem we know, but to the spiritual Jerusalem. The writer of Hebrews said,

> You have not come to something that can be touched... But you have come to Mount Zion and to the city of the living God, the heavenly Jerusalem...
> — Hebrews 12:18, 22

We know that Isaiah's ultimate vision was of "new heavens and a new earth" (65:17). Jesus Christ established the spiritual City of the Lord in his redeeming death and resurrection. As Paul wrote, "So if anyone is in Christ, there is a new creation: everything old has passed away; see, everything has become new!" (2 Cor. 5:17). That City of the Lord exists where God's people gather in his name. Though largely hidden now by brokenness and the results of human sin, the City will be revealed in its fullness in God's future.

The City of the Lord is a current spiritual reality. At the same time, it is yet to be revealed to humanity in its fullness. It is part of that mysterious "already and not yet" created by the work of Christ (which we began considering in chapter 6). Already the City has been established; not yet has the full vision been enacted. So we live hoping, striving to pull the "not yet" down from the future and into the present world. We struggle in this life to realize that this world is not all there is. There is much more to come, and we try now to keep alive the vision of God's realm. "For here we have no lasting city, but we are looking for the city that is to come" (Heb. 13:14).

Here, we may draw a comparison with the way new housing developments are sometimes marketed today. One model house may be built and landscaped so that potential buyers may see more clearly what the new neighborhood will look like. Similarly, the church universal is the prototype of a house in the kingdom of God. We are the artist's rendering of the community that is to be developed. God, as the "developer," desires to show the world through us what can come to be. The better a model we are, the more likely that the world will "buy into" God's planned community. So, we are to pattern our life together after the community of the redeemed, which is yet to be fully revealed.

PEACE AS YOUR OVERSEER

Life in the City of the Lord will be characterized by an absence of violence and destruction. The harmful behaviors that perpetuate the cycles of abuse and crime will be stopped. For the needs underneath the actions will have been met. Steady, reliable love will replace the fear of abandonment. Attention will be given instead of neglect. Joy will rise above despair. God will fill the vacuum into which we previously tossed—to no avail—wanderlust, shopping binges, too much to drink too often, power moves, and a thousand other kinds of stimulants.

The people in exile who had Babylonian overlords heard that their new taskmasters will be Peace and Righteousness (60:17). The rule of the day will be the things that make for peace. Honesty in business and fairness in trade will make the daily exchanges in the marketplace joyful. Instead of the rush of greed there will be the satisfaction of equity. Every citizen will feel valued, and all contributions to the common good will be celebrated.

The New International Version says that Peace will be your "governor." This makes me think of the governor on an engine, the mechanism which regulates the machine's speed. In God's City, then, peace will regulate my urges to overreach. Righteousness will make a border around any impulse I may have to get more for myself at the expense of others. There will be a balance among the citizens that will lead to a deepening wholeness and sense of well being among the entire city.

Moreover, this external atmosphere of peace and goodness will be internalized by the citizens: "Your people shall all be righteous" (60:21). We will act righteously because we will be righteous. The presence of the Lord and the gift of his redemption will recreate us from the inside as well as rule over us from the outside.

A CITY OF KNOWING

Another characteristic of life in the City of the Lord will be clear knowledge. Now, as Paul said, "we see in a mirror, dimly" (1 Cor. 13:12). Today we doubt. The evidence of the world seems stacked against our hope. God's love is such a quiet force amidst the racket of contemporary life. We feel God in one moment but lose the sensation in the next. It is difficult to sustain fervor in worship and faith, but in the City vision will be clear: "You shall *know* that I, the LORD, am your Savior and your Redeemer, the Mighty One of Jacob" (60:16, italics mine).

We will know because God will be directly present among us. There will not be the wavering in our perception of God's reality. Rather, the light of God's presence will replace the sun as the source of our illumination, warmth, and ability to see:

The sun shall no longer be your light by day,
nor for brightness shall the moon give light to you
    by night;
but the LORD will be your everlasting light,
and your God will be your glory (60:19).

God will make his dwelling place among us. We won't be playing a guessing game anymore about where to find the Lord. The age old questions of faith will be resolved. What has been hidden will come to light. At last, everything will make sense. And God's love and grace will be directly perceived by all within the City.

As a result of God's presence, the prophet said, "your days of mourning shall be ended" (60:20). The book of Revelation deepens this vision when it adds, "God himself will be with them; he will wipe every tear from their eyes. Death will be no more; mourning and crying and pain will be no more" (Rev. 21:3-4). This is a glimpse of heaven.

Through the resurrection of the Redeemer, Jesus Christ, the power of death has been broken. Though we still feel its sting now, in the City of the Lord such grief will be assuaged. Though creation still seems "subjected to futility" and in "bondage to decay" (Rom. 8:20-21), then it will be made new, restored to the glory God intended in the beginning.

The City of the Lord will be a place of everlasting life. The vision in Isaiah formed the basis for the highest view of what is to come that the church possesses. One day, we will live free from sin and death, glorying in the presence of God. We will not need to struggle to take our new names. Rather the people of that City "will worship him; they will see his face, and his name will be on their foreheads" (Rev. 22:3-4). We will bear God's name as our defining identity. And that name will give us everlasting joy.

DEMONSTRATING THE CITY IN THE CHURCH

As the community of God's people, we will be named the City of the Holy One. As with the other names, we may take the identity before it is fully realized. It becomes our goal. Based on the work of salvation accomplished in Jesus Christ which assures the future fulfillment, we strive now to offer the world a model of life in that forthcoming City.

The church today invites the presence of God in our worship. The more open our hearts and the more total our devotion, the greater the experience will be of the presence of God. We struggle now to enact the justice of the future City in our present dealings. We labor to regard people first as beloved children named of God, looking beneath other titles and names given by the world. We submit ourselves to the taskmaster Peace and the governor Righteousness. They command in us now a higher loyalty than even the world's insistent demands.

Bearing such a name, we move through our days aware that we are citizens of another country. Our true home is in God's realm, not on this present earth. The way things are is not the way things will always be. Though it hardly seems possible now, we cling to the hope that God's City will be established in the gift of the new heavens and the new earth. Our work is to live by the customs of the new City before it has fully come to be.

In this way, the church draws the world to God. We hold forth not a condemning, but a welcoming word. All nations are invited to come to this City. And the quality of our interactions as a community will be a stronger witness than our words. The vibrancy of our worship will be a beacon of light that draws people home from the long darkness they have endured.

We take the name "City of the Lord" as we see ourselves called into relationships with one another that demonstrate the values of the City to come. Living by such a vision, we have a great hope to hold forth amidst the deathliness all around us. The more we live out this name, the more we will sustain our faith in such a future, and the more we will experience the presence of God as illuminating every aspect of life together.

CHAPTER 13

YOU SHALL CALL
YOUR WALLS SALVATION

You are the light of the world.
A city built on a hill cannot be hid.
— Matthew 5:14

One aspect of the City of the Lord deserves special attention. In fact, Isaiah added a new pair of names which apply to the boundaries the City. We read, "you shall call your walls Salvation, and your gates Praise" (60:18). The issue of protective boundaries seems to be of high importance. Yet, it is curious to me that this City even has walls and a gate. After all, if everyone is coming there, why have any fortifications?

To consider this question, I returned to my days of building sand castles. I have always preferred to create walls and entrances rather than the buildings themselves. Perhaps this only attests to my level of skill—or lack of it. Yet, amidst the vast, formless sands of the beach and before the surging, rising waters of the ocean, the walls provide definition to the city within. They encompass the castle grounds and so set them off from the rest of the beach, opening them to further embellishment.

Walls make entry into the city an event. We have to gain passage through the tunnels or across bridges and over the moats. Probably we have to rearrange our possessions in order to fit through the gate. And certainly, then, we know when we are actually within the city itself. The walls and gates make it clearly defined.

The City of the Lord cannot simply collapse its walls and tear down its gates, for then it would cease to have any definition apart from the rest of the world. And Isaiah makes it clear that those thousands who stream joyfully to the city are making a definite choice to leave one place and enter another. They are bringing the best that they have and offering it to God as part of their admittance to the Holy City.

Entry into the City is a radical change in life. It feels like a homecoming, like a dove returning to its nest. But coming home means leaving other places behind. And the pilgrims know when they have entered. The people are in a profoundly different community. Here, the very walls of the City magnify the sound of the worship within.

But how shall we describe these walls and gates? We might say that the walls around a city or castle are imposing. Or formidable. They say "Do not try to enter here by force." Or they might appear weak, in a shambles, ready to fall down. Likewise, the gates may be rusty and stuck. Or they may fairly shout, "No admittance without permission." Ordinarily the fortifications, while providing definition, also dissuade intruders.

But these walls in the City of the Lord are named Salvation. The fortifications imply, then, "Come inside here and be safe. This is your refuge. These walls enclose a place of peace. People upon their ramparts are watching for your arrival, urging you on, wishing you to find what your heart longs for within." A ring of houses in the City are built right up against the walls for protection. But bricks and mortar do not provide the security. The steadfast, continuing love of God creates the circle of safety.

And the gate of the City of the Lord always stands open. Its name is Praise, for entering one is immediately aware of the loving presence of God. Passing through the gates of the City of the Lord evokes a response of joyful praise: "Alleluia! Here is home. Here is God whose light shines in the darkness. Here is the community of the just and the righteous. Here is a city of peace. Praise be to the Lord!"

The walls and the gates of this City are inviting and attractive. Passing through them is the entry into a new and fulfilling life. But, and this is crucial, the City of the Lord nevertheless maintains walls and gates which define it over and against a world full of darkness.

THE WALLS OF THE CHURCH

As we saw in the previous chapter, the church universal is the prototype of the City of the Lord. The church has a defined story and message which may not be changed. These are its walls and gate. All are invited to come within these walls to see the splendor of God. Barriers of economics, class, race, beauty, health, strength, intelligence, or sophistication all must be torn down. But one barrier remains. Entrants must recognize the Lord of the City; they must bow to the lordship of Christ.

Those who enter the City bring tribute and acknowledge the glory of the Holy One of Israel, the one God who alone is Lord of all. The tribute offered is the symbol of the offering of one's life in service to the Lord. Passing through the gates is acknowledging the reign of God. Jesus said "I am the gate. Whoever enters by me will be saved, and will come in and go out and find pasture" (John 10:9). Through the gate of Christ is life and salvation. But to enter, one must change, leaving the old life and embracing the new in order to be part of the City of the Lord. No other basis for exclusion exists. But this one exclusionary clause is inseparable from the vision of Isaiah and the biblical faith.

These demands may at first seem harsh. How can we be so insistent that others believe as we believe? How can God who invites everyone be so choosy about faith? Yet it makes more sense if we reverse the charges. How loving would we be if we knew what makes for grace and life and then withheld that knowledge? If God has entered history in his revelations to his people, and particularly through his incarnation in Jesus, how can we not tell of that tremendously good news?

To keep secret the new names from God for fear of imposing our beliefs leaves the lost from ever learning that they are Sought Out. The unwelcome and unlovely cannot learn how they are God's Delight. Those who have gone a long way down roads of destruction cannot be called home without our voicing the call of God. Silence about what has been made known to us would be the cruelest message of all.

When Jesus declared that he was the gate, he did it as protection for the sheep from robbers and poachers. The purpose in his boundaries is one of life. He added to the passage quoted above, "The thief comes only to steal and kill and destroy. I came that they may have life, and have it abundantly" (John 10:10). Our walls and gate are not meant to restrict but to protect and enhance life.

In the days when our culture was suffused with Christianity, there was little distinction between Christians and the general public. We all breathed the Christian ethos whether we subscribed to the faith or not. Now, as culture becomes more diverse, the message of Christianity appears more pointed. As culture grows more secular and individualistic, the City of the Lord stands in sharper relief against the background of the world.

We realize that we have a story to tell and a name to name. Two quotations, one from this century and one from the fifth century express this enduring theme. Bishop Lesslie Newbigin, in his book, *Truth to Tell: The Gospel as Public Truth*, discusses what it means to have a faith based on a revelation that occurred in history:

> The central claim of the gospel, [is that] Jesus, the crucified and risen Jesus . . . is alone the center around which alienated human beings can be drawn together in a reconciled fellowship.

> We have a gospel to proclaim. We have to proclaim it not merely to individuals in their personal and domestic lives. We do certainly have to do that. But we have to proclaim it as part of the continuing conversation which shapes public doctrine. It must be heard in the conversation of economists, psychiatrists, educators, scientists, and politicians. We have to proclaim it not as a package of estimable values, but as the truth about what is the case, about what every human being and every human society will have to reckon with. When we are faithful in this commission, we are bound to appear subversive. I think the Church cannot evade the sharpness of this encounter.[8]

---

[8]Lesslie Newbigin, *Truth to Tell: The Gospel as Public Truth* (Grand Rapids: William B. Eerdmans, 1991), 64, 61.

Making a truth claim does indeed create a sharp encounter in our pluralistic culture. It throws up gates and walls. The walls of the church are made of the story of a God who promised a Redeemer and then sent one in Jesus Christ. God has come among us, and offers healing love and a new creation. This news changes the way we look at everything. The City of the Lord will be revealed in the future. That hope has a profound affect on the way we consider how to order this world now. And so we will clash with the forces which wish to maintain the structures of unbridled greed, free choices for destruction, and unchecked domination of the weak and powerless. If we maintain our walls and our gate, then the people of the world have a place to go for refuge.

TELLING THE STORY

The second quotation is traditionally attributed to Saint Patrick, who brought the gospel to Ireland. The Celtic religion on that island included an awareness of the spiritual nature of the world. The Celts believed there could be a god of the river and a god of the sky. There was great individual latitude for aligning oneself with a particular god. They lived close to the earth, and much in their religion was admirable. Patrick used every connection he could make with the ancient Irish beliefs. And then he jumped from there to proclaim the uniqueness of the gospel message. He responded to a query from two princesses about the God he served:

> Our God is the God of all, God of Heaven and earth, sea and river. He has his dwelling in heaven and earth and sea and all that are therein. He inspires

all things; He quickens all things. He kindles the light of the sun and the moon. He has a Son, co-eternal with Himself and like unto Him. And the Holy Spirit breathes in them. Father, Son, and Holy Spirit are not divided. I desire to unite you to the Son of the Heavenly King, for you are daughters of a king of earth.[9]

Can you feel the power in his preaching? He does not insult nor does he rave. He appreciated the religion of the two daughters, but at the same time he did not simply leave them where they were. He did not say, "Whatever you want to believe is up to you." Rather, with loving concern, Patrick vigorously preached the story of Christ. He proclaimed the truth and the greatness of God and let the Holy Spirit do the convicting. Patrick invited the two women to enter the gates of praise for the God of gods, to come within the walls of salvation and enjoy the City of the Lord.

As Christ's church, we have an identity called forth in the new names, which we are not permitted to change. Our work as a community is to receive and enact these new names from God. Then, our community is to be patterned after the City of the Lord that is yet to be. Our walls should be walls of salvation and deliverance. Our gates, our doors, are to evoke praise. Here, the light of God is to shine like a beacon to a world in darkness. And we should be on the ramparts and in the streets inviting others within.

So we have to ask a series of questions of our particular churches: "Coming into this community, do people hear the sounds of praise which magnify the Lord? Or does it sound

---

[9]Found in David Adam's *The Cry of the Deer* (Wilton, CT: Morehouse-Barlow, 1987), xiv.

hollow, as if we are embarrassed to proclaim the news we have? Do these walls communicate salvation? Can people come here and drop their baggage and realize that they have come home? Who among us are standing on the ramparts urging the wanderers to come in ? Who among us are going out as scouts to bring home the lost? Who is binding up the broken so they can make it here? Who is assuring the unlovely that they have a place of honor? Who will tell the sinners that they are welcome among this collection of sinners who have found forgiveness? Can people learn their new names here?"

All barriers between us and the world are to be destroyed save one. This is the wall of salvation which defines the gospel given to the church. This is the gate of praise for the living God which defines the life of the redeemed. This barrier we may not compromise, for the very life of the world depends upon it.

So let us set the walls singing with the story of salvation. Let us call the world by the new names God promises. Let the banners fly high so all can see. Let us stand at the gates blowing trumpets of invitation, to come in, to come home, to the praise of the one Almighty God who walked among us in Jesus Christ, the promised Redeemer who calls us by name!